SEE THE END FIRST

BOB CRUMLEY

SEE THE END FIRST

3
Simple
Yet
Difficult
Rules Of
Success

Advantage®

Published by Advantage, Charleston, South Carolina.
Member of Advantage Media Group.

ADVANTAGE is a registered trademark and the Advantage colophon is a trademark of Advantage Media Group, Inc.

Printed in the United States of America. 2nd Printing

ISBN: 978-159932-372-5
LCCN: 2012950485

This publication is designed to provide accurate and authoritative information in regard to the subject matter covered. It is sold with the understanding that the publisher is not engaged in rendering legal, accounting, or other professional services. If legal advice or other expert assistance is required, the services of a competent professional person should be sought.

Advantage Media Group is proud to be a part of the Tree Neutral® program. Tree Neutral offsets the number of trees consumed in the production and printing of this book by taking proactive steps such as planting trees in direct proportion to the number of trees used to print books. To learn more about Tree Neutral, please visit www.treeneutral.com. To learn more about Advantage's commitment to being a responsible steward of the environment, please visit www.advantagefamily.com/green

Advantage Media Group is a leading publisher of business, motivation, and self-help authors. Do you have a manuscript or book idea that you would like to have considered for publication? Please visit www.advantagefamily.com or call 1.866.775.1696

TABLE OF CONTENTS

9   FOREWORD *by Steve Gilliland*

13   INTRODUCTION
       The Power of Three
       Simple and difficult are different things
       My history with success

25   CHAPTER ONE: HARD WORK WILL EVENTUALLY PAY OFF
       What do you want?
       Why don't more people "see the end first"?
       How do I start figuring out what I want?
       Plain old hard work
       Break the work down
       How long does all this work take?
       Work may lead you to something unplanned

63   CHAPTER TWO: CONSISTENT COMPETENCY IS BETTER
       THAN ERRATIC EXCELLENCE
       Don't drive for excellence too soon
       How do we become competent?
       Use goals and plans to find the competencies you need
       Identify the necessary core competencies and master them
       Competency and excellence are moving targets

93   CHAPTER THREE: NEVER GO INTO THE RING WITHOUT THE
      WILL TO WIN

        Rings as symbols

        Focusing on why

        Have multiple passions and ambitions

        Fear or excitement?

        Don't let fear rob you of the start

        Balance your passions

        Help your people find their passion

        How do I find my passion?

        Passion is not enough

        Summoning Elvis and the will to win

        Be like Elvis and Jamie

        Learning the right attitude

        Help your attitude by eliminating retreat

        Celebrate victories and honor those who succeed

        Cheating isn't winning

125   FINAL THOUGHTS

131   ACKNOWLEDGEMENTS

FOREWORD

A FRIEND AND FAN

One day, Bob Crumley called me and asked if we could get together for lunch. I almost always decline these kinds of requests, since I simply don't have the time. However, since Bob's brother, Lance, is a good friend of mine, I agreed to a meeting at a restaurant in Clemmons, North Carolina.

Bob and I connected immediately. We had a great discussion about our families and life in general. The first thing I noticed is that he was smart—*really* smart. He understood how to connect with people. What's more, he wasn't just smart, he was wise, too. His passion and daring spirit fascinated me. A licensed attorney, he has been a county manager and county attorney, a human resource executive and corporate ideas guy, a 40-percent owner of a managed healthcare administration company, and, most importantly, a pizza delivery boy for Domino's.

THE IMMEDIATE BOND

The first thing Bob shared with me is that he saw life differently. He didn't see it better, just differently. As I listened to his stories, I began to realize the similarities of our thinking patterns and everything we had in common. We shared a way of thinking that generated revenue, solved problems, and created opportunities. His evident humility and generosity were a complete breath of fresh air.

SIMPLE AND EASY ARE NOT EQUIVALENT

"Sometimes the simpler something is, the more difficult it is to master," Bob states in his book. That's just a sample of the common sense and realistic inspiration you'll find in this informative and practical book. It gives readers a refreshingly wise and workable prescription offered through three simple yet difficult rules. In his book, Bob tells us about "the power of three" and provides answers to help you achieve a balanced and successful life. He reinforces how to recognize and understand what you want and what it looks like when you get there. He also helps you realize that achieving your goals will take the hardest and most important work you will ever do. Plus, Bob shows you how to achieve those goals by following his Three Rules: 1) hard work will eventually pay off; 2) consistent competency is better than erratic excellence; and 3) never go into the ring without the will to win.

GAME CHANGER

Since reading *See the End First: Three Simple Yet Difficult Rules of Success*, I have sought to incorporate Bob's three principles into my life. Bob's ideas have deepened my philosophy and passion, which is helping people make a life: developing the artistry of living. In fact, I have taken the material in this book and used it to generate ideas that are now incorporated into my company's guiding principles.

I urge you to read this book, study it, and implement the Three Rules into your personal and professional life. For example, write a business plan for your family; by doing so, you'll give people the leadership they need and deserve. My wish is that you begin to develop a philosophy of life based on these rules, a framework upon which you can build an even more solid foundation. Doing so will lead to success and significance in every area of your life. I truly believe that all of us are here to make a difference—and that difference happens when we're able to get our lives together. If you value any type of success and you really want to achieve it, it requires hard work, really hard work.

ENJOY THE RIDE™

I can't remember the last time I enjoyed a book as much as this. You owe it to yourself to read *See the End First: Three Simple Yet Difficult Rules of Success*, apply its wisdom to your own life, and share its message with those who matter most to you. This beautifully written book will touch your soul and inspire you.

Are you disoriented about your direction in life? Are decisions tough to make and steps hard to take? If so, you're in luck. Bob Crumley has created a masterpiece of wise counsel that you can consult. *See the End First* is more than a book. It offers a perspective that will reduce your stress, simplify your decisions, help you find your passion, increase your satisfaction, and, most importantly, help you *enjoy the ride!*

Steve Gilliland, *Bestselling Author*
Member, Speaker Hall of Fame

INTRODUCTION

Trust me, I didn't start out in life determined to write a book about success. If you polled my high school classmates, they probably would have pegged me as the last guy to write anything. I wasn't a member of the Honors Club, a class officer, or a BMOC (big man on campus). Though I worked hard, I didn't have an overarching direction for my life. There were successes, but colossal failures. I went from being homeless in my thirties to semi-retiring at age fifty-two. And, how happy I am that the judgment of my early peers was not the determining factor for my life.

This is probably not the first self-help, motivational, or career development book you have read. You may have started out with books like *How to Win Friends and Influence People, Think and Grow Rich*, or *The Seven Habits of Highly Effective People*. Yet you may have found, as I have, that most books detailing success principles are way too complicated. This conclusion is not the product of scientific, psychological, or even literary analysis. Rather, it is a conclusion derived from the complexity the authors use to describe what's involved when working toward success. Sometimes it feels as though an author makes the subject complex so we can see the value of the book.

I became overwhelmed by the difficulty of these texts when I saw a book containing 282 success principles. That's right: 282! How in the world can that strategy work? I bet most of you can't name the Ten Commandments in order. (I have tried that little test on a lot of people.) Can you name all 50 states? How about all of your cousins, nieces, and nephews?

Yes, we have the capacity to remember and analyze lots of stuff. However, if we are trying to learn something and use it on a daily basis, holding on to 282 principles seems like a bit much.

During my early years of seeking success, I discovered books, ideas, and concepts designed to help people move forward. Sometimes one of them would come to the surface, but often not. Then, one day, I stumbled across the rules set forth in this book practically by accident.

This realization wasn't sexy, it didn't take place during a dream, and it wasn't the result of years spent comparing books about success. Instead, I found my inspiration on a hot summer day at a hot, sweaty, and smelly horse show.

My oldest daughter, Brandi—we call her "B"—was competing along with her large pony, Amie. This was the last class of a two-day show, and Brandi was in the lead for Grand Champion. All she had to do was get a single ribbon. It didn't matter if that ribbon was for first or last place. Even so, she rode terribly. She was obviously off her game, more interested in that big Grand Champion ribbon than the specific ribbon for the class she was riding. She did end up getting a ribbon, but it was for last place.

As she rode out of the gate, after the ribbons were awarded, the look on her face was one of disappointment, not joy. Although she was Grand Champion, she knew she had not ridden like a champion. As she and her pony came over to where our family stood, she was clearly struggling with overwhelming emotions.

Without warning, quietly and without emotion, the following words came out of my mouth. I spoke as though I had rehearsed these words for years, even though they had never crossed my mind before: "B, there are only three rules for success in this world. First, hard work will eventually pay off. You have worked your butt off to get here. Second, consistent competency is better than erratic excellence. Third, never go into the ring without the will to win. In this last class, B, you violated rule number three, and that's why you feel bad."

Today, Brandi doesn't really remember me giving that little speech. She has heard me tell this story several times—and she has heard these rules many times since—but she doesn't remember that speech on that day.

But I do. Once I'd said those rules, I couldn't put them out of my mind. All my years of struggle, successes, and failures had finally and succinctly rolled up into those three little rules of success.

As I continued thinking about these rules, I realized they were not the Ten Commandments. They were not 282 success principles that would have taken until dark to lecture poor B about. Instead, they were three simple, yet difficult, rules of success. I could remember them. I could understand them. Most importantly, I could *live* and *work* with them because of their simplicity. Notice I'm not saying they are easy; they are simple.

As time passed, I used these rules as the basis for my businesses and my life. I told them to my children, Brandi and Jamie (JJ). I repeated them to the folks at the office, and I mentioned them to friends. Several friends asked if I would speak to their employees or salespeople about these rules and how they changed my life. So I did. Over and over, people kept saying to me, "You should write a book."

I listened. I started to write a book. As any author might, I began to share parts of my book and ideas with folks who knew me and whose opinion I trusted, including Arnie Malham. After I described my philosophy and book to him, he summed up the overarching theme of my beliefs and this book in just four words: "*See the end first.*"

With those simple words, he wrapped all my years of experience into a neat little package: a powerful, meaningful, and success-ensuring package. I told Arnie he was a genius. Actually, I think my exact words were, "You're a freakin' genius."

After reading this book, you'll be able to see the end first, too. As we go through the Three Rules and how they work in our lives, keep a close eye out for this overarching theme. It is critical to success and makes up the foundation for these rules. Once you've mastered them, you can apply these rules anywhere. They aren't just for moneymaking enterprises. They work just as well for marriages, education, personal development, and even horse shows.

When I began *See the End First*, I'd never written a book before. I wanted my readers to get an immediate, not an eventual, payoff from this book. So, I asked my good friend, author Robb Grindstaff, to work with me as I wrote this book. Robb is a really cool, very accomplished guy who's had a long career in the newspaper industry as an editor, publisher, and executive. He has worked for small-town newspapers, large metropolitan newspapers, and as executive editor of *Stars and Stripes*, the U.S. military's newspaper. Now retired from journalism, Robb writes novels and short stories; he also edits books for various authors from around the world. In the case of this book, Robb is more than just an editor. He is my friend. As you will see later, he and his family lived part of this book's events with me and mine.

Robb and I want to keep this simple. In this introduction, we discuss the book's title, the power of three, and the difference between simple and easy. Then, the rest of the book is divided into three sections, one for each rule. While we address each of them separately, you will see the rules together several times throughout this book, too. We want you to learn them and commit them to memory. We also want you to take them to heart, verbalize them in your daily life, and be able to spot any violations of them. Moreover, we want you to teach these rules to your kids, exemplify these rules in the workplace, and use them to help you reach whatever dreams and goals you set for yourself. In short, we want you to use these rules in your daily life and *live* them.

THE POWER OF THREE

After the Three Rules first spilled out, I began to analyze what I had said to B. While this analysis didn't happen at the horse show, it started on our drive home and continues even today. Recently, when I was being my usual Type-A self in yoga class, my instructor used one of my own rules on me. When I stopped laughing, I understood that she had taken the rules I had taught her and was using them to teach me. What a great moment!

So, how did I begin my analysis? What I saw first in the rules was their simplicity. By this I mean they are easy to remember and easy to verbalize. Rule One is the "what," Rule Two is the "how," and Rule Three is the "why."

However, why just three rules? Why not four or five? Why had my brain synthesized all I had read and learned into three specific rules? As I pondered this, I began to see the number three more and more in people's lives, in our psyches, and in everything around us.

- For example, Aristotle talked about three and the ability of humans to relate to it in his book *Rhetoric,* when he wrote about *ethos*, *pathos*, and *logos*. Can you believe he wrote this in the third century B.C.?
- There are three primary colors.

- Americans have three branches of government: legislative, judicial, and executive.
- Sigmund Freud said we are id, ego, and superego.
- John Alan Lee, Ph.D., opines that there are three primary styles of love: *eros*, *ludos*, and *storge*.
- Psychologist Robert Sternberg has written about the triangle of love as involving intimacy, passion, and commitment.
- Julius Caesar famously said, "*Veni, Vidi, Vici* (I came, I saw, I conquered)."
- We're surrounded by safety warnings like "Stop, Look, and Listen" and "Stop, Drop, and Roll."
- Literary works, like *The Three Little Pigs*, *The Three Bears* (with a little Goldilocks thrown in), and *The Three Musketeers*, are full of threes.
- The Christian faith celebrates the Trinity of the Father, Son, and Holy Spirit.
- Finally, Benjamin Franklin divided "[h]umanity […] into three classes: those who are immovable, those who are movable, and those who move."

Everywhere we look, we see things divided into threes. In fact, about a year or more before I uttered the Three Rules for the first time, I had written a business plan for my family—that's right, a business plan for my family—that I'd separated into three parts. In this plan, I saw the end first: I focused on where I wanted to take our family and where I wanted us to be financially. (I'll get to *why* I constructed this plan later.) My plan had what I called the "three-legged stool" of finances: one "leg" represented our primary law firm business, the second represented our real estate holdings, and the third represented our securities. I planned to develop each of those three areas to give our family financial security. If one leg was wobbly, the other two could hold up our finances overall until we could fix that leg. This method has worked well for us.

At the time this book was written, the real estate market was experiencing a major downturn. Our law firm, while feeling the recession's effects, remained strong, and our securities had ridden the waves of this latest recession well. Perhaps that's because our law firm is also based on a three-part foundation: we offer three primary services. In addition, this rule of threes extends throughout our financial plan: our real estate company has three investment areas (residential, office, and retail buildings), and our financial investments are in cash, stocks, and bonds.

When I developed that family business plan, I was operating in what I see as a "triangle of power"—the power of three—and I didn't even realize or understand it. I do now, though. Why fight what our brains are meant to do and how they are meant to do it? Something in people intuitively understands, relates to, and operates best in an environment of threes. Let's use that reliance on threes to our benefit. Let's develop ourselves with that understanding and power.

This concept does not limit us. Rather, it empowers us. We can use the concept of three in multiple permutations. We're always able to come back to the strength of three, just as light always comes back to the three primary colors.

If these rules are so simple, then, why does success so often elude us? It eludes us because the execution of these rules, following them in our day-to-day living, is difficult. Believe me, I know. For example, I have been thinking about this book for years, but I struggled mightily to find the consistent competency I needed to write it.

SIMPLE AND DIFFICULT ARE DIFFERENT THINGS

Simple: not ornate or luxurious; unadorned
Difficult: not easily or readily done

To explain the difference between the concepts of *simple* and *difficult*, let's use some examples. Losing weight, for instance, is simple: eat less, exercise more. How hard can that be? Yet for some people, losing weight can be difficult. For instance, try walking past the roasted-corn vendor at the state fair, not pausing to investigate as he dips a golden ear into melted butter. Maybe a treadmill makes the perfect clothing rack. When I thinking of all the things I have tried to accomplish, maintaining a healthy, reasonable weight has been the hardest.

Similarly, saving money can be difficult but should be simple. You want to accumulate wealth? Don't spend all you make. No sweat! It's simple: income is what you make, but wealth is what you keep.

Wait a minute, though: you expect my family to watch the Super Bowl on a 43-inch wide screen when they just came out with a 60-incher? My daughter can't ride a broken-down pony now, can she? All the while, I sip my $4 latte and listen to my digitally downloaded song on my latest, greatest smart phone. In the meantime, my investment and retirement accounts sigh with loneliness. Go to the grocery store and buy fresh ingredients for cooking a healthy meal at home? Nah! Why don't we just grab some fast food? Eating fast food is a great idea if your goals are to gain weight and lose wealth.

> **GOLDEN NUGGET**
> *It's simple: income is what you make, but wealth is what you keep.*
>
>

We all could think of many other things that are simultaneously simple and difficult. Just because something is simple does not mean it is easy. Sometimes the simpler something is, the more difficult it is to master.

Each of the three apparently simple rules has two kinds of difficulty within it: the difficulty of each rule's various moving parts and the difficulty of living by that rule each day. I guarantee you will find one of the rules more difficult to follow than the other two. What's more, you will find your ability to match the rules' difficulty with simple adherence ebbs and flows. For instance, you may be spot on in following Rule One, working hard toward your eventual payoffs, but you may have to strive mightily to follow Rule Two and be consistently competent.

For me, Rule Three is the most difficult to follow: it's hardest to find the attitude and will to win. I have a mercurial personality. Some days I am up, some days not so much. Some days I am ready to tackle the world, and some days I am rebounding from the world tackling me.

Which rule will be your hardest to master? Which will be your best? Think about this as you explore the rules in this book.

MY HISTORY WITH SUCCESS

When I talk about these rules in public, I always ask permission to speak about "the good, the bad, and the ugly" parts of my life. I want permission to talk about the bad times and the good times—to have permission to speak about when my family was homeless and also about how I became a millionaire. I want to do both without you feeling sorry for me or without you feeling I am boasting too much. At seminars, I ask for that permission publicly. So, if you don't mind, will you give me permission to speak freely and openly to you as you read this book? Out loud, please!

Thank you.

Why would you want to read a book about how to be successful from someone who has not been successful? Here's where part of that permission comes in.

I am a serial entrepreneur. Sometimes I feel this quality makes me like royalty and sometimes just one step above a serial killer. It took a lot of years to fully realize that I am, at my core, an entrepreneur and I just see life differently than folks who are not entrepreneurial. I don't see life better, just differently.

I grew up poor, living on a farm in Tennessee and then in a North Carolina small town. I have worked since I was five years old. I worked my way through college and law school. I worked for a large savings and loan association and took an assignment in Washington, D.C. Soon after, I became one of the youngest county managers and county attorneys in North Carolina's history: at age twenty-five, I was responsible for 350 employees and a $16,000,000 budget. Next I launched a retail business, and then I launched a financial services company. I married my sweetheart and had two beautiful daughters.

Then my family and I lost everything. We lost our house. The banks wouldn't take our cars back, and we lost what little savings we had. We were homeless until my wife's family took us in. I delivered pizzas until I landed a job as a law firm's junior associate. There, I served as a starving attorney until I got back on my feet.

So, why might you want to read a book about what I have to say about success?

Today, my wife and I own a law firm with more than 130 employees in sixteen offices in North and South Carolina. Our real estate development company holds two shopping centers, seven office buildings, four apartment complexes, two rental houses, more than eighty-one acres of land for development in six locations, and a car wash. Finally, we own a music publishing company in Nashville, Tennessee. Whew! That's a far cry from being homeless in 1987.

While most businesses took a hit during the Great Recession, all of our businesses and investments are riding out the turbulent times and, as I'll discuss in detail in later chapters, are doing even better than before.

Early in my career, I had gained a degree of what some would call success, but it did not make me happy. It was not what I wanted. I was a hard case who had to lose it all before I could focus my mind and my heart on what I truly wanted in life. Only then was I willing to slow down, think, and see the end first. I had to put my three simple yet difficult rules into daily use in all aspects of my life—family, business, and self-development—before I found the results that met my personal definition of success.

By learning and applying these simple rules, you too can achieve the success you want. First, you have to know what you want. You have to *see the end first*.

CHAPTER ONE

HARD WORK WILL EVENTUALLY PAY OFF

1 👁

HARD WORK WILL
EVENTUALLY PAY OFF

Consistent competency is better than erratic excellence
Never go into the ring without the will to win

When you first read this rule, I bet your mind went straight to your tasks—that is, to a list of the actual physical and mental chores with which we are all so familiar. Whenever I give a talk about the Three Rules, I always ask the audience members what they first think of when they hear me say the phrase, "hard work." Invariably, they answer with a list of specific tasks.

Hard work is made up of tasks, but while tasks are important, they are by no means the most important aspect of Rule One.

I have never been afraid of hard work. I launched my first entrepreneurial endeavor at the age of five. It was 1962, a bumper year for corn in east Tennessee, and my grandfather had a corn patch. I proposed a deal. If he supplied the corn at no cost, I would supply the logistics, sales, marketing, and accounting. Of course, I didn't use those terms. Hey, I was only five. As I put it then, if he would help me pick the corn, I would put it in my Red Flyer wagon, haul it around the neighborhood, and sell it door to door. We would split the proceeds evenly.

The plan worked. I was in business. Later, I went door to door with my grandfather, selling a truckload of peaches he had bought in South Carolina. At each stop, I watched as he held a peach in one hand and showed it to a potential customer. He slowly opened his pocketknife and then, even more slowly, cut a slice of that peach and let the customer see the juice run out. From him, I was learning to sell the sizzle, not the steak.

As I grew, I kept working. We had no local paper, but at age eleven I obtained a paper route for *Grit*, a national paper sold by local youth within their neighborhoods. I earned five cents per paper. For me, selling in my "neighborhood" meant taking a mile walk to the nearest housing subdivision. I would work those houses and then go to the nearby commercial airport to hawk papers. In the summer, I sold my customers flower and garden seeds. In the fall, I sold them Christmas cards.

By the time I was twelve, my paper sales had grown to five hundred copies a week. Including sales of my other products, I made as much as $50 to $60 a week. Remember, this was 1968-70.

When I was thirteen, my dad's job took our family to North Carolina. I soon landed stable employment in a restaurant. Always looking for a side business, I also washed my boss's cars, a Lincoln and a Thunderbird, which he soon let me drive. Talk about a reward! Fourteen years old and I got to drive those cars. Okay, I only got to go about fifty feet from one side of the lot, where the cars were parked, to the other side, where I cleaned them. I would have done it for free, just for the driving thrills, but my boss paid me.

I worked in restaurants until I graduated from high school. In the meantime, I developed two more side business deals.

My first side deal found inspiration one day when I heard two local businessmen talking about how copper was going to be in short supply. One of them joked he should start hoarding pennies. Unlike today's pennies, pennies back then were primarily made of copper. I thought, "Hmm, why not?"

I began to take part of my restaurant paycheck to buy pennies—lots of pennies. Sure enough, when the public shortage scare came, I had a cottage business selling pennies to the town merchants. While this wasn't a huge business, it taught me about supply and demand, risk-taking, and pricing strategies. If I set the price for a hundred pennies too high, the merchants would not buy. Instead, they would choose to give customers change rounded up to the nearest nickel. If I charged the right price, I made money, the merchants saved money, and the customers got exact change.

My second side deal emerged during the gas shortage in the early 70s, when long lines of cars would sit for hours at gas stations. I opened the business of "car-sitting" in line at the gas station. I didn't have a driver's license because I wasn't old enough. Still, my hard work and experience driving that Lincoln and Thunderbird across the restaurant parking lot was paying off. For a dollar an hour, I would sit in someone's car, holding the place in line and inching the car forward as the line moved. The customer would come back later, when his or her turn at the pump came closer.

This way, I got a dollar an hour to sit in a car and listen to the radio. Hard work, indeed.

During college and law school, I moved out of the entrepreneurial game but kept working. In college, I served as resident assistant and student government officer; during my third year of law school, I waited tables. To this day, I consider a potential lawyer who has waitstaff experience as a better candidate than one who has had no direct customer service jobs. You haven't learned true customer service until you've been paid with tips.

At this point, I had spent most of my early years hard at work, accomplishing tasks. That's what hard work is, right? Finishing tasks. That's what I thought. And hard work pays off, right? It had paid off for me when I was pushing corn, developing a paper route, washing cars, and sitting in gas lines. As a young lad, I learned the value of hard work and earned spending money. I valued hard work as its own reward.

> **GOLDEN NUGGET**
>
> *Hard work toward achieving an objective is not the same as working hard to complete tasks.*
>
>

However, there were some lessons about hard work I hadn't yet learned. As Rule One says, hard work will eventually pay off. But hard work toward achieving an objective is not the same as working hard to complete tasks.

I would soon learn that lesson too, and like many of life's lessons, it came the hard way.

After law school, I took a job at a savings and loan association as in-house counsel. At my new job, two things soon smacked me right in the face.

First, the real world can and often does change, and *your* world can be rocked or torn apart. Second, I was not cut out to work for other people or to know exactly how much money I would make (no more, no less).

Within a year of taking that job, my employer sent me to Washington, D.C., to work for a short time with a law firm that specialized in savings and loans (S&L). At that time, the S&L industry was undergoing deregulation, and the unintended, or perhaps intended, consequence of that deregulation forced many into bankruptcy. This was the early 80s, when interest rates for a home loan were about 16 percent. My assignment was to research and write a legal paper about how to define bankruptcy for a mutually owned company.

Talk about a wake-up call.

I was miserable. Internally, I was motivated: I wanted to do a good job, an excellent job. Yet the worst day of my month was payday because I knew how much I would be getting ahead of time. Although it would be a while before I would declare myself an entrepreneur, I struggled with the concept that no matter how hard I worked, no matter how many hours I put in, and no matter how exceptional the quality of my work, my reward would always be exactly the same.

Some of my law school classmates told me I had succeeded— that I had made it. However, my situation did not feel successful to me because I did not know what I wanted. I didn't know what success looked like.

WHAT DO YOU WANT?

It does not take much strength to do things, but it requires great strength to decide what to do.

–Elbert Hubbard

Each man must look to himself to teach him the meaning of life. It is not something discovered: it is something molded.

–Antoine de Saint-Exupéry

The most important aspect of Rule One, which also happens to be the part most people never do, is to ask, "What do I want? What do I want my relationships to look like? What do I want my business to be? What does it look like, taste like, smell like, feel like when I have achieved what I want?" People never stop to see the end first.

I'm not talking about coming up with an easy answer like, "Well, I just want to be successful" or "I just want a happy marriage." Seeing the end first is much more than that. We often fail largely because we start out on our endeavors without truly knowing what it is we want or what success looks like to us. If you don't know what you are after, how will you know when you have it? More likely, how will you know that what you have isn't what you're after?

I graduated from law school, passed the bar exam, landed a position with a large firm, and got an assignment in Washington, D.C. Yet I was an utter failure because all this apparent success didn't fulfill what I wanted. I had never really thought about what I wanted my life to look like.

In these early years of my life, I did not know this truth about goals. I had broad goals, including the following: I want my own business, I want to be financially successful, and I don't want to be poor any longer. However, these were not concrete goals. They had no accountability processes, no timelines, and no measurement systems. They weren't really goals. They were just dreams.

I want to say that again. An idea is only a dream, not a goal, until you write it down, make it concrete and measurable, and build accountability systems to help direct you to the desired result. Developing an accountability system can be as simple as telling your goals to well-meaning, honest friends and asking them to help hold you accountable, or as complex as hiring a personal coach or joining a fully functioning best-practices group.

GOLDEN NUGGET

An idea is only a dream, not a goal, until you write it down, make it concrete and measurable, and build accountability systems to help direct you to the desired result.

When the S&L industry ship started sinking in the early 80s, I was offered a job as county manager and county attorney. This job helped me make many good connections.

Richard Petty, the NASCAR driver, was one of the county commissioners. He sat right next to me at commission meetings. About a year and a half after I started that job, some guys I went to church with got permission from the top eight NASCAR drivers to retail licensed apparel. This included the license for Richard's name and likeness.

At that time, the only place you could buy licensed merchandise was at a NASCAR racetrack. This opportunity would be the first time merchandise would go direct to retail in a sport growing in popularity, and we all knew it.

I wanted in, so I negotiated the T-shirt and hat part of the deal; the others kept the golf-style shirts, coats, and other apparel.

After negotiations, I was on cloud ninety-nine. NASCAR was going mainstream and I was part of it. My ship had come in, and it was a Petty blue racecar with the number 43. This was my ticket to wealth and success. No more little deals, I thought. This would be the real deal. The big deal.

Yet the big deal had one small problem. I had no money.

A textile company in our town made millions of T-shirts. Problem solved. I put together a business plan and set up an appointment with the owner and executives. I pitched the idea that their firm should invest $250,000 to help get my dream started.

They were as excited as I was, so off we went. We designed the shirts and hats, and landed J.C. Penney to sell them in stores throughout the Southeast. The investor company manufactured our shirts under a private label and outsourced our hats.

Guess what happened then? Nothing.

Launching a business idea ahead of its time can be just as much a failure as starting up a buggy whip company the year after the Ford Model T rolled off assembly lines would have been. Our sales were terrible. We were ahead of the market, ahead of the big NASCAR boom, and ahead of off-track apparel sales. NASCAR fans bought their shirts and hats at the track as souvenirs. Folks who didn't go to the races weren't interested.

We went through the $250,000 in about six to eight months. By then, it was apparent this product line was going nowhere. We liquidated our stock at fairs and festivals. We were out of business.

I had quit a great job as county manager. I had a wife, a child, and a busted company. Then the company owner, David Stedman, called. He wanted a meeting.

Before I left for the meeting, I joked to my wife, Teresa, "I think involuntary servitude has been outlawed in America." I got myself together and left.

After I arrived, the receptionist ushered me into David's office. It was not really that fancy considering he was a guy with more than two thousand employees.

He looked up at me and said, "So, how are you doing?"

"Well, the merch isn't selling, we're taking back loads from Penney's, and—"

He interrupted me mid-sentence. "I didn't ask you about the business. We can talk about that later. How are *you* doing?"

I didn't know what to say. I stammered a bit and finally answered, "Well, not so good. Business is shot, I'm out of a job, and I've got a wife and a small child."

Next, he said some magical words. These were words I had never heard before, but they hit my heart and soul the moment he said them.

"Bob, you're an ideas guy. I need ideas guys. I have lots of guys to do the work. I need ideas guys." He paused to let me soak that in for a moment before he continued. "The business idea was sound. We went back over it before this meeting. It just didn't work out. We lost our money."

At least he hadn't said, "We lost our shirts."

In that moment, he could have said one of two things. He could have said, "How are you going to get that money back?" But he didn't.

Instead, he said, "I want you to join our company. I want you to spend time coming up with ideas about how to make us better and how we can grow."

I wasn't in a position to be choosy, but to make conversation, I asked what this job entailed.

"I don't know what jobs we have, but my HR department will find you something. I just want you to come up with ideas. Oh, and I want you to have a 10 percent raise over whatever we were paying you for this shirt business."

Even though I had just lost $250,000 of his money, he wanted me because I was an ideas guy. Plus, I got to pick my job and I got a raise. This was not exactly how I had thought our conversation was going to go.

David picked up the phone, called HR vice president Bob Warren, and told him, "Bob Crumley is coming to work with us. Find him something to do where he can come up with ideas."

I have always wondered what must have been running through Bob's mind on his way to David's office. I imagine it went something like this: "Let's see, Crumley loses 250K of the boss's money, but the boss likes Crumley. Crumley is an ideas guy, and he's coming to work with us. Hmm… I think I'll put him in HR."

That's what happened. I became the Director of Personnel Services in charge of compensation and benefits. Lest you think I knew nothing about this subject, rest assured I had some experience. When I was county manager, our team had instituted the first countywide personnel system and we had redone all the salary scales and benefits. At least I knew something. Technically, I was qualified for that position.

That evening, I walked into my house.

"How did it go?" Teresa asked with a bit of trepidation. She was worried about my mood and wondering just how bad things were.

"In case you didn't know it," I said, "you are married to an ideas guy. The boss gave me a job and a raise. I start tomorrow."

Without hesitation, Teresa said, "That's not the least bit funny. What really happened?"

I take two lessons away from that day. First, I had always been an ideas guy; I just never gave myself credit for it. Second, sometime during your life you will have the opportunity to either crush someone or lift that person up. Which you choose says more about you than it does about the other person.

> **GOLDEN NUGGET**
> *Sometime during your life you will have the opportunity to either crush someone or lift that person up. Which you choose says more about you than it does about the other person.*

David lifted me up that day. He gave me something worth more than a job and a raise: he gave me a renewed belief in myself when I needed it badly. I have never forgotten that day. In fact, my memory of it has often tempered my actions when someone in business has not performed to my standards or an idea has gone south.

My tenure at the textile company lasted only about two years. Although that was a relatively short time, I learned a lot. When a new CEO couldn't get some long-term staff members to buy into why he was brought on board, he restructured the company. Some employees only knew the company's old-line methods, and their heads turned around and around when the CEO brought in new, updated manufacturing systems. Some of these folks did not understand the world was changing and international competition was breathing down the necks of every U.S.-based textile company. Instead, quite a few folks buried their heads in the sand. However, the new CEO knew this truth, the company owner knew it, and I was learning it. This environment was loaded with learning opportunities for an ideas guy.

Why did I only last a couple of years, then? Because of an idea! The mid-1980s saw the start of managed care for employee benefit plans and the expansion of some benefits for employees, like COBRA. The days of just buying a company-wide health insurance policy and hoping for the best were coming to a close. Our company, which had about two thousand employees, was self-insured. We paid a big insurance company about $200,000 per year just to administer our plan, handle the claims, and pay the bills. After considering the situation, I thought this could be a good revenue start for a new business. My boss, the Human Resources VP, and I developed a strategy for our company to start a new, smaller company that would administer the larger company's healthcare plan, along with other companies' plans. We took the idea to the CEO and the executive team, and they agreed.

My next company was off and running. I just didn't own any of it.

About a year into the process, in 1986, the CEO informed me that the larger company was being sold in a leveraged buyout, but the new owners didn't want the "healthcare thing." I had six weeks to buy out the company or it would be shut down. Acting quickly, I found a money partner at another firm with which we had been doing some business. Together, he and I bought the company.

After the failure of the T-shirt business, my wife and I had found our footing again. We started 1987 in our first home. We had two car payments, a nice savings account, pristine credit, and our second child on the way.

That year, I learned another very valuable lesson about Rule One's concept: "Hard work will eventually pay off." Sometimes, when you have investors that control your company, their timeline for "eventually" does not match yours. From painful hindsight, don't own 40 percent of a small, privately held company, especially when the idea for the company and its vision are yours. In about a year or so, I had taken the company to over $1 million in sales, but we were chewing up capital.

In June, my partner came into the office and said, "I want more control of this company. You are not the president anymore."

We were on the cusp; our company was growing and I saw great opportunity ahead. Unfortunately, our opportunity didn't match my partner's needs or his vision for his money. The end I saw and the end he saw did not match up, so we were done. Our parting was not the most amicable, since I was left holding credit card bills for company expenses and without insurance for our second daughter's birth. My family and I can laugh now about "mortgaging" Jamie for three years as we paid off the hospital and doctor bills.

By the end of the year, our savings were gone, we had to sell our house, and the bank didn't want our cars back. Taking all we had with us in a small U-Haul truck, on Thanksgiving Day we moved in with my wife's parents near Chapel Hill, N.C. Talk about not feeling it when the Thanksgiving prayer was said! We had no money and our credit was shot.

I was more devastated than I had ever been in my life. My in-laws are wonderful people, and they made things as comfortable as possible, but you can't build a house big enough for two families. Although we were staying with them, I felt homeless. I had to have a job, any job, so I went out looking the very next Monday.

I found work almost immediately and easily in Chapel Hill. After all, I was a licensed attorney, a former county manager and county attorney, a former human resources executive and corporate ideas guy, and a former 40 percent owner of a managed healthcare administration company. I found a job the first day I looked.

I became a pizza delivery boy for Domino's.

Every day, I delivered pizzas and prayed no one would find out I was a lawyer. One day, a few fellow employees were talking about a legal matter. They had it all wrong. Without stopping to think about it, my inner lawyer kicked in; I told them how it really worked.

They looked at me in amazement.

"How do you know that?" one of them asked.

I quickly recovered and stammered, "I… I… I don't know. I guess I heard it somewhere." Whew, the remaining shards of my dignity were safe for a few more days.

After the huge failure of 1987 and our homelessness, I understood that if I wanted to be successful, I needed to define and understand what the concept meant to me—not to others, but to me. I needed to slow down my actions and think about the end first. I needed to understand what I valued in the long term and not just concentrate on the short term.

That concept became reality when I created my family business plan, which I mentioned earlier. I developed the thought process for that plan during my thirty-minute commute back and forth to work. During those quiet times, with no radio on to distract me, I allowed my mind to plan, to think, and to feel. I'm not recommending you try this while you drive, and I try not to do it anymore either. At least I didn't have any accidents!

What I do recommend, and what I often do now, is simply to get in a dimly lit room with no TV, stereo, Internet, or any other distractions, and just think about what you want and what is important to you. I am not just talking about financial success. My rules for success are universal. They can apply to marriages, sports, business, household finances, school, and any other endeavor in which you seek success.

As you think about what you want, write your ideas down without judgment or discernment. When you have thought out what you want fully—in other words, when you've determined what success looks, feels, tastes, and smells like to *you*—take another look at your list and begin the winnowing process of reconsideration. This is not a one-sitting job. This is a process that should take several hours across several days. Take the time to determine within yourself what it is you truly want.

Recently, at fifty-five years old, I started doing yoga. I weighed 250 pounds, my waist measured forty-two inches, and I was terribly out of shape. I didn't go to that first yoga class with a firm goal in mind. I was on vacation, so I dropped in on a class just to get some exercise and to explore something new. While part of me had always wanted to try yoga, another part of me had prejudged it. I thought yoga was all sitting around, murmuring "om," and twisting body parts into a pretzel. I quickly learned practicing yoga is a way to use your body to heal itself, your soul, and your mind. Besides, you are straining so much not to fall on your butt that you don't have time to say "om" very much!

Within a week, I had fallen in love with yoga. I could see the physical, mental, and spiritual impact it was having on me. (There's the concept of dividing things into threes again.) Yoga wasn't like the other dreadful exercise or running regimens from my past. This practice soothed my soul and energized me. I could see myself doing it for the rest of my life.

While on vacation (in fact, while I was writing this book), I began to use this rule's technique of asking, "What do I want?" I thought about this question, in relation to yoga, for a week or more. As I considered the topic, I talked with the vacation resort's instructor, Diego, about what yoga could do for me physically and how my body should react to the work. We discussed yoga's mental and spiritual sides. I learned the physical changes would come first. As I grew excited about the physical changes and learned to control everything in the moment, including my breath, the mental changes would follow. Finally, if I diligently worked and slowed down long enough to allow my soul to think and feel, I might achieve the spiritual changes.

In terms of my physical goals, I decided becoming limber, strong, and trim ("LST," as I call it) was right for me. That is, I would invest the work into yoga and it would give me back an LST body. This type of body might not be right for everyone, but I decided it was right for me. I started visualizing what having an LST body meant. In my mind, I can see my waist slim, my chest open, and my legs strong as I bend forward and touch my nose to my shins. I can see it, I can taste it, and I can feel it. This transformation has not fully happened yet. However, in just five months, I have lost thirty pounds and six inches from my waist. My instructor here at home says she can see the striations of my deltoids when I am in the downward dog position. When she first said that, I didn't know I had any striations, let alone in my deltoids. I quickly checked to make sure I hadn't split my pants.

In addition to illustrating a point, I have a couple more reasons for telling you this story. First, when I meet you, I want you to be part of my accountability program. I want you to ask me, "Bob, how is that LST stuff going?" Second, and more importantly, my real point is to let you see how I use these rules every day. If I can do it, so can you. Using these rules applies equally to yoga and to building a business.

WHY DON'T MORE PEOPLE "SEE THE END FIRST"?

Why don't more people simply take the time to ask themselves what they truly want? Well, to answer that question requires real self-introspection and self-knowledge. Doing so requires that we value some things and devalue others. Most folks do not want to totally, publicly state their values. They don't want to cast some things aside, or label them as not meaningful, because they are afraid someone, most likely someone they know and maybe love, will look at them with disapproval. Instead, they are more comfortable living lives of quiet desperation, knowing they are not moving toward what they want or, even worse, *not* knowing what it is they truly want, than they are risking the disapproval of others.

If you value any type of success, including financial success, and you really want to achieve it, you must be prepared to put in hard work.

> **GOLDEN NUGGET**
> *If you value any type of success, including financial success, and you really want to achieve it, you must be prepared to put in hard work. Really hard work.*

42

Really hard work. What's more, you will pay a price for success. For example, in the early years of building my law firm, I did not have time to make a lot of friends. I didn't have time to join local clubs or hang out in the lawyers' lounge at the courthouse before court. Because of that, I paid a price with the bar association and with many in my town.

However, I made these choices because I had examined myself and my life. During that examination, I put a higher value on my family's financial security than on my social life. I wanted my girls to go to better schools, for instance. If that meant some of my fellow lawyers made fun of me and ostracized me, then that was that. I knew what success meant to me.

I didn't make this choice because I wanted to be rich without friends. While my company was on the road to a goal of success, my business friends, mentors, and peers were not necessarily in my town. My friends, these lawyers and other professionals, lived in Connecticut, Kentucky, Tennessee, Texas, California, Washington, and a host of other states. I made this choice because I had to decide what I wanted most. When I made up my mind, my decision told me and other people what I valued and what I didn't.

This internal valuation process keeps many people from taking the time and the effort to decide what they really want. Yet answering that question is the cornerstone to your true success.

HOW DO I START FIGURING OUT WHAT I WANT?

As you sit and ponder these questions of what you really want and what success looks like to you, you must embrace the things you value. You must discard the things of lesser value in order to reach your goals. Most are unwilling to do this valuation process and winnow down their lives. In fact, many people will toil and sweat, working hard until their bodies can't take any more, without ever asking "Is this really what I want to do?" For them, completing the sweat, the work, and the tasks is easier than facing themselves, their values, and, in the end, their hearts.

If you want to succeed, you must not fail to do this work. It is critical. It is the foundation for all the other work you will do. As many wise people have said, find work you love and value, and you will never really work a day in your life. When you see the end first, the tasks you do will be filled with an understanding of where they fit in your life and what you are working to accomplish.

No one can tell you how this aspect of answering this question, and following your first rule, will come out. I can only give you hints about how to approach it until you decide what you really want.

Let me give you one more hint through another example from my own life. When I first thought about building my own law firm, I explored a lot of legal areas. I looked at criminal, domestic, real estate, bankruptcy, and personal injury law. Even though I thought I could apply the strategies and tactics I had learned the hard way to grow a firm in any of these areas, I chose personal injury because it involved medicine.

Why medicine? My mom, Jane, was a registered nurse. Her medical books always intrigued me, and I often read them when I was a teenager. I had participated in gross anatomy dissection along with medical school students while I was in law school, and Mom had even received permission to let me scrub in and participate in an appendectomy. My participation was limited to holding a retractor, but I was still in the room, next to the surgeon. That was such a cool experience. Given all these factors, as I was thinking about what I wanted—what I wanted this new company to look, smell, and taste like—the clear edge went to personal injury because it involved medicine.

Next, I had to decide what kind of personal injury law to practice. Should I take on huge cases or small-to-large? What is the difference?

A business acquaintance of mine, who lives in Ohio, handles big medical cases. When I last spoke to him, he had about twelve cases on his docket and was working out of his home. He had a line of credit established, and during the years when no cases resolved, he lived off that credit. Whenever one of his big cases settled, he paid off the line of credit and made great money.

Why was this lifestyle good for him, and why did he value it? My friend wanted to be a stay-at-home dad and spend as much time at home with his kids as he could. His values drove the way he built his business and how he would work.

But that type of business would drive me crazy. I wanted a law firm equivalent to a business like McDonald's, one at which you have some customers and some income every day. Every now and then, a big bus pulls in and you have a great day. My personality is better suited to a business that has some consistency, more even cash flow, and some new customers every day. That's the kind of firm I built.

Now, ask yourself versions of these questions. What do you want? What fits you and your personality? Fighting for success against your nature is a recipe for disaster. It is hard enough to be successful in any endeavor when the odds are with you, let alone when you are fighting against who you really are.

GOLDEN NUGGET

What do you want? What fits you and your personality? Fighting for success against your nature is a recipe for disaster.

After you do the hard work and find out these things about yourself, you'll be able to say, "This is what success looks like for me in this endeavor." Can you taste it? Can you see it before it becomes a reality?

Conducting this visualization, what I call "seeing the end first," is so important. It helps your mind create the vision. It allows you to see what success looks like before that success becomes a reality. It conditions your mind to understand success in this endeavor is possible because you can already see it and, in your mind, you have already experienced it.

Athletes use this process of visualization probably more than any other group. They spend time before an event visualizing—or "pre-playing"—the day and their upcoming performance. They make sure it links up with the model they have been visualizing during their training.

"But, Bob," you say, "can that work for me and my business?"

Why not? I know it will work for you because it works for me. I pre-play every meeting beforehand. Before setting any goal, I spend time thinking about what reaching that goal means, what it will look like, and what it will feel like when we attain it.

In the early stages of a visualization, I do not worry or think about how we are going to reach the goal; I only focus on what it looks like when we do and how we will feel. In many ways, your mind cannot distinguish a vivid, emotional thought from an actual event. When someone pre-plays an event in his or her mind and is willing to see, feel, and taste the emotions of the end result, his or her mind can go to work more easily to fill in the blanks of achieving this already experienced event.

Remember, deciding what you want and understanding what it looks like when you achieve that want is the hardest work you will ever do, but it is also the most important work you'll do on your journey through the Three Rules. *You must see the end first!*

PLAIN OLD HARD WORK

Now the really hard work is done, let's get on to just regular old hard work. There is no success in any venture without hard work. Period.

It amazes me how many people will say things like, "Man, I wish I had your money."

I always respond, "When do you want to start putting in fifteen years of twelve- to fifteen-hour days?"

When they don't answer, that's when we understand their wish is just that. They wish a genie would come down and give them financial security, an LST body, or a 3.5 GPA, but they are not willing to work for it.

Many seek to minimize the work my company did do by saying how lucky we are. To be sure, luck does play a part in anyone's success. However, I've heard and believe this truth: "The harder I work, the luckier I get."

Consider the story of the master pianist, who mingled with some people after his show. A member of the audience came up to the pianist and said, "I'd give my whole life to be able to play like you."

The wise pianist said, "I did."

No one in that recital hall had seen the hours he had practiced, experienced the stiffness of his overworked fingers in the morning, or felt the loneliness of that practice room for days on

> **GOLDEN NUGGET**
>
> *A member of the audience came up to the pianist and said, "I'd give my whole life to be able to play like you." The wise pianist said, "I did."*

end, year after year. Of course, they didn't get to feel the warmth of the applause on his face or the satisfaction of knowing Mozart or Beethoven would be proud of his interpretation of their hard work, either.

In my case, once my wife and I started the law firm, we worked twelve- to fifteen-hour days, six to seven days a week for a long, long time. Oh, we loved the work, knew we were on the right path, and learned new and exciting things every day. Still, those days sure got long, and we paid some prices for them.

Earlier I mentioned the price we paid with my local peers, but our kids also paid a price. When my youngest daughter, Jamie, was writing her college applications essay, she wrote that she did not remember falling asleep in her bed at home when she was growing up. She remembered falling asleep at our law firm. When their after-school care was over, the kids would come to the firm, and Teresa or I would get dinner and bring it to the office. Teresa did the accounting, marketing, and advertising; I managed the business and handled cases. We would eat, and then the girls would do homework while we did more office work. After that, they would play with the computers or phone system before falling asleep. While Brandi was partial to the couch in the waiting room, we often found Jamie under the front office manager's desk.

Reading her essay brought tears to my eyes. Immediately, I wondered if we had paid too high a price. Had they paid too high a price? She saw the look on my face and, being a perceptive young woman, said, "No, Daddy, it wasn't bad. It was great. You were teaching us that it took hard work to be successful. Besides, we had cool stories to tell at school about how we got to play on the computers and phones."

What did they learn from this experience? My eldest daughter, Brandi, worked long, hard hours at her horse trainer's farm while she was in middle and high school, and she achieved her goal of going to the National Finals. Now a college graduate, wife, and mother, she still loves horses. She is passing that love and her knowledge of hard work along to her son, Colton, all while she builds her own business as an Arbonne consultant and works for our real estate company.

Jamie, who sang for the Queen of England along with her high school chorus, graduated first in her class from her university. She is a talented singer and has moved to Nashville, fully prepared for the hard work required of a country music artist.[1]

Both my daughters understand the value of hard work. They have seen what it is like and what it can do for people and their families.

Now, let me share some hints about how to make it through all that hard work. First, as mentioned above, do something you value, something you love. Second, when you come up for air, remind yourself of the end you saw first, how much you value it, and how much you love it. Hard work is not fun every day. By its very nature, it can't be. Whether you get bogged down in the tedium of making sure all your office tasks are done correctly or stuck in suffering through another set of yoga exercises, sometimes your ultimate goal will be all you have to carry you through.

Focusing on your ultimate goal, along with not wanting to hear your accountability folks question why you are not following through, will help motivate you during those dog days of plain old hard work.

---

1 Check out www.jamietatemusic.com. Sorry, this proud father couldn't resist!

BREAK THE WORK DOWN

Break your work into manageable and discernible tasks. This way, you can mark off your path to success more easily. As an example, in our firm we have a rule that a lawyer must call his or her clients at least once every month. This call must take place whether there is something to talk about or not. Because of the types of cases we handle, some months the lawyers just wait and nothing really happens.

When I worked cases as a lawyer in my firm, I did not always have time during the day to make these routine calls. I was too busy building the business, seeing new and current clients in the office, attending court hearings, or calling clients about urgent issues. Guess what the number one complaint about lawyers received by bar licensing boards across the nation is? They don't return calls.

So, what was I to do? Break down the tasks. I made Tuesday nights my call-the-clients nights. I would eat dinner at the office and then get on the phone to call clients. I would not go home until I had made those calls. By making that simple task decision, I got my routine calls made in one marathon evening each week.

After I began making my marathon calls, something else started happening. My clients started telling people, "You won't believe who called me last night at 9:30. My lawyer!" They were bragging to their friends about how their lawyer was working and calling them at 9:30 at night. How do I know? I know because my clients' friends told me so when they called me to sign up their cases at our firm. I felt great. I was getting that discernible, simple task of calling my clients done, plus I was marketing our firm at the same time. That's what you call a win-win!

People recognize when you work hard, go the extra mile, and are fully committed to your success, no matter how you determine what that success is.

HOW LONG DOES ALL THIS WORK TAKE?

Remember that Rule One explains hard work will *eventually* pay off. For me, this concept has been the hardest part of the rule to grasp and appreciate.

Now, more than ever, we live in a want-it-now, get-it-now, have-it-now world. This mentality is a large part of why, years later, our nation and the world are still reeling from the 2008 recession. We have forgotten that sometimes we have to delay gratification to obtain it, that good things come to those who wait, and that self-indulgence breeds national indulgence, which leads to economic disaster.

Most of the successful people I know have not experienced overnight success. My wife and I have not, but many people I meet seem to think so. What they see as an "overnight success" is that person's current status, the star he or she has become, or the financial success he or she has today. However, these onlookers never see the struggle. In most cases, they don't want to see or hear about that struggle because it doesn't fit into their mentality of waiting for a lucky break and experiencing that type of quick success, too.

> **GOLDEN NUGGET**
>
> *We have forgotten that sometimes we have to delay gratification to obtain it, that good things come to those who wait, and that self-indulgence breeds national indulgence, which leads to economic disaster.*

Let's look at a few examples, starting with Garth Brooks, a huge superstar who burst onto the scene in the 1990s and became an overnight success. Right?

In actuality, Garth toiled in Nashville for many years, honing his skills and his craft. He worked various day jobs to supplement his meager musical income. He made some money singing demos (demonstration recordings). A music publisher trying to promote a song will give a demo to an artist and a record company as an example of what that song could sound like. The publisher hopes the artist and company will like the song, do a master recording of it, and release it to the buying public and radio. That way, everybody can make some money. Nashville session musicians, who are the envy of the recording world, usually play the music for these demos, and a demo singer sings the words.

Back when Garth was starting out, he sang demos for my music publishing company partner, Lane Caudell, and for many other publishers as well. Lane recalls his company paid Garth fifty dollars a song. Imagine this: the man who has filled huge venues, had one of the largest concerts in New York City history, and who has a constantly sold-out solo show in Las Vegas, was singing demos in Nashville for fifty dollars a song. Lane still has many of those demos and sorely wishes he could release them.

As a second example, take Colonel Harland Sanders of Kentucky Fried Chicken fame. At age forty-four, Sanders was selling fried chicken from his gas station. After he moved to a restaurant location, the governor awarded him the title of Kentucky Colonel because of how good that fried chicken was. At sixty years old, Sanders closed his restaurant because he had a bigger dream and a bigger idea. He would sell the rights to his cooking method and his recipe for great chicken to others, and he would get a nickel for each chicken they sold. He was sixty and had been cooking chicken for over sixteen years. Finally, Kentucky Fried Chicken was born; ultimately, this company became a worldwide brand and made Sanders a millionaire.

For a third example, consider the case of Ronald Reagan. As many readers might remember, Reagan was what many consider the greatest president of our lifetimes and perhaps one of the greatest of all time. He did not run for elective office until he was fifty-five. He also made two unsuccessful runs for the presidency before being elected. When he took office, he was sixty-nine, the oldest president ever. Reagan had an abiding faith that hard work would eventually pay off. He was on a path he knew was right for him, even when his party and his nation were not quite so sure. Through all this, he persevered. An entire nation, and indeed the entire world, will forever be grateful that he did.

So, that's one example from the arts, one from business, and one from politics. How about one from my life?

My daughter Brandi was about nine years old when she fell in love with horses. This love started at a Girl Scout camp with a simple horse-riding course. Brandi was hooked. She was in love. When she got back from camp, she wanted to continue her lessons and did so at a farm about ten miles from our house. During that summer, Teresa and I would drop her off at the horse farm before going to work in the morning; many nights, we picked her up after dark. Brandi badly wanted a horse, but we wanted to make sure this passion was going to stick before we spent money on what could be a passing fancy.

Frequently, she would come home, head straight to her room, and fall asleep on top of her bed in those smelly horse clothes. She would get up the next morning, still in the same clothes, and go do it all again. She was emulating what she had seen. She was working hard at something she loved and knew was right for her.

A year and a half later, she got her first horse: a large pony named Amie. Amie and Brandi walked, trotted, cantered, and jumped their way to that fateful day when she would ride for the championship, which was also the day when I spoke the Three Rules for the first time. Her hours and hours of work on hard, sweaty, summer days and cold, shivering, winter days had turned into beautiful ribbons representing her success. These ribbons still hang in our home, ever a reminder of her work.

Brandi wasn't done. One night, when she was in the eighth grade, she announced she had something she wanted to talk about after dinner. Now, when your thirteen-year-old daughter tells you she has something she wants to talk about after dinner, a lot of things go through your mind. Most of them are not good. As I recall, that dinner was over pretty quickly. Brandi made the situation even more maddening by asking her little sister to leave the room. Oh my God, I wondered. What was coming?

After Jamie had exited, Brandi reached below her chair, pulled out a brochure, and said, "You know I want to go to the Nationals. The competition is not the strongest here. So, this is where I want to go to high school."

As she handed us the brochure for an all-girls school in Massachusetts, I breathed a sigh of relief. I can assure you that discussing her high school education was not where I had thought that conversation would be going.

Brandi was serious and had done her research. She had selected one of the top three riding schools in the nation, which happened to be a great academic school as well.

A year later, we dropped off our fourteen-year-old at a boarding school in Massachusetts. If you had told me when she was born that I would end up agreeing to let her go to boarding school, I would never have believed it. It's still hard to believe today. Yet it was her dream and her goal to make the Nationals, and her plan was both doable and reasonable.

In the big leagues of high school competition, she quickly learned she had a lot of catching up to do. Many of these girls had been competing since they were six or seven, and Brandi hadn't started riding until age nine. However, during her four years there, she received the Most Improved Rider award several times; she ended her senior year by receiving the Most Valuable Rider award.

Most importantly, Brandi achieved her ultimate goal of making the Nationals. She didn't win. Long ago, she had understood the magnitude of just making it, so she had set her eyes on that difficult but attainable goal and made it happen. To put this achievement into perspective, by the time she arrived at Nationals, Brandi had worked almost one-half of her life to make it there.

"Eventually" can be a long time coming. It was for Garth Brooks, Colonel Sanders, President Reagan, and Brandi. I am sure there were days when each of them wanted to give up. I know I have had days like that. Yet they persevered. If you want to be truly successful, you must resist the urge to quit. You must have faith in yourself and in your success. You must recognize that the work you do now will lead you to the first rule's final aspect.

WORK MAY LEAD YOU TO SOMETHING UNPLANNED

A harsh reading of this section on hard work may lead you to believe you should just continue to work hard, even if something is not working. However, isn't doing the same thing repeatedly while expecting a different result a common definition of insanity? Sometimes we just need to cut our losses, as tough and painful as that may be.

I had to cut my losses in both the NASCAR T-shirt business and the healthcare administration business. Those were tough and painful times. What I know now, but didn't then, is that through those failures I was learning valuable lessons about business, about myself, about partners, and about what to do and not to do.

GOLDEN NUGGET

There is a fine line between quitting too soon, before your dream has a chance to fully develop, and recognizing when it is appropriate to move on.

There is a fine line between quitting too soon, before your dream has a chance to fully develop, and recognizing when it is appropriate to move on. David Stedman, the owner of Stedman Corporation and my investor in the NASCAR T-shirt business, taught me that lesson when we met.

David said, "We have analyzed it again, and everything was right in our earlier analysis. Do you feel we have given it an appropriate amount of time and test?"

Everything in me wanted to scream, "No, let's not give up." However, I knew it was time. We needed to cut our losses and move on. We had tried different sales models and different types of stores. The shirts just weren't selling. We were a few years ahead of a market that has now developed into a multimillion-dollar industry.

Sometimes, though, instead of quitting and moving on, we need to step back, look at a broader vision of who and what we are, and redirect our efforts.

In the early 1980s, for example, the Norfolk and Southern Railway folks had some decisions to make. The rail business wasn't all it had been, but their company was profitable and throwing off lots of cash. To be successful in the long run, they realized, they couldn't just be in the railroad business. They had to reinvent themselves as part of the transportation business. Among other reinvention tactics, Norfolk and Southern bought a large stake in the profitable and growing Piedmont Airlines. A little over five years later, Norfolk and Southern sold their stake in Piedmont to US Air for what have been described as "huge profits." Those profits, along with profits they made in other industries, helped Norfolk and Southern grow even stronger in their original railroad business.

Unfortunately, many people don't do the hard evaluations and make the hard decisions in their lives or businesses until their current models have totally failed and they are out of cash. I've seen this firsthand in the textile and the furniture businesses. I've watched some companies burn through all of their cash and borrowing capacity while trying to hang on to a dying industry.

Of course, there are exceptions, like the Acme-McCrary Corporation. Acme-McCrary is a thriving textile company in my hometown. When most of the other textile companies were going out of business, Acme-McCrary's executives beefed up their research and development team and found niche markets in which they could build their business.

You may have heard of a product that filled one of those niches: Spanx.

Sara Blakely, the woman who came up with the idea for Spanx, had gone to several manufacturers, but could not find anyone who would take a chance on an untested entrepreneur and an untested product until she met the folks at Acme. Today, her product and company are valued at more than $1 billion, and Acme has been there with her every step of the way, both in R&D and in manufacturing.

On a personal note, at our law firm, the current recession has caused us to reexamine our core case offerings and move into some new areas. I owe a huge "attaboy" to our executive team for recognizing developing issues in our core businesses. Those issues, which were outside of our control, were making our firm's future not so rosy. The executive team examined each of our offerings to make sure we were maximizing our efforts. Then they developed two new case areas, which are beginning to make up a significant portion of our company workload and revenue.

Whether the right decision is to call it quits and move on or to redirect, often the lessons you learn will lead you into areas about which you never would have dreamed. I bet Ronald Reagan didn't envision becoming President of the United States when he landed his first acting job. Yet getting that job led to him becoming the president of the Screen Actors Guild, which led to him doing speeches, which led to him becoming Governor of California, and, ultimately, which led him to the presidency of our nation.

Colonel Sanders started out making chicken in a gas station. I bet he didn't spend time thinking, back when the hot grease was mixing with the humid summer temperatures, that his face and name would be branded all over the world one day.

When I was in law school, if you had told my classmates and me that I would own a statewide injury law firm and be part of revolutionizing the practice of law in my state, no one would have believed you. However, the lessons I learned from putting in hard work on my other businesses and jobs, and in my failures and successes, led me to a place from which I could see an opportunity and the way to capitalize on it.

Once you have done the hard work of seeing the end first and deciding what you want, and after you have developed your strategies to achieve that end, be willing to work hard. Very hard. I can't guarantee that all your efforts, especially in business, will be successful. Sometimes you have to be willing to cut your losses and move on. However, sometimes the base, or the groundwork you have done, will lead you into an area you did not anticipate. This may be the area where you will find your ultimate success.

> **GOLDEN NUGGET**
>
> *Once you have done the hard work of seeing the end first and deciding what you want, and after you have developed your strategies to achieve that end, be willing to work hard. Very hard.*
>
>

People have been finding value in their groundwork for hundreds of years. In Renaissance Italy, for example, glassblowers would inspect their blown-glass art. If they found imperfections, the glassblowers would set those pieces aside and rework them into flasks or wine bottles. These usable bottles were, perhaps, not art, but were valuable just the same. The Italian word for flask? *Fiasco.*

Sometimes, as you travel the hard road of success, your fiascoes turn out to be valuable, too.

In retrospect, my fiascoes (including the failed healthcare administration company, our homelessness, and delivering pizzas) redirected me to the success I had sought for so long. In December 1987, while pushing pizzas, I secured a job with a law firm. I was scheduled to start in January 1988. The firm wouldn't let me start until after New Year's because of tax- and expenses-related reasons. I waited and delivered those pizzas. Every time I drove up the driveway of my in-laws' house, I felt like a failure. It was nothing my in-laws or my wife said; it was just how I felt. My two girls deserved better.

The last week of December, we moved back to our hometown so I could start with the law firm on the first of January. We didn't have much money, but I had a friend, Bill Boyd, who owned some apartments.

Bill, who had been chairman of the county commissioners when I was county manager, went on to become a member of the North Carolina General Assembly. He was one of the kindest and most generous men I have ever known. A few years ago, I was honored to be one of the six who carried him to his final rest.

Back in 1987, he told me, "Bob, I have an apartment on the north side of town. It's not big, but it does have two bedrooms. You guys can live there as long as you want. Pay me the rent whenever you can."

Over the years, Bill and his wife, Shirley, often took my family out to eat. Many times, they gave us a fifty dollar handshake.

Once I asked Bill how I would ever repay him. He said that one day I would be wealthy and in a position to do the same for somebody else. By doing so, I would be paying him. (This was years before the movie *Pay It Forward* came out.)

We moved into that small apartment, and I started working for the law firm. I was thirty-one, had started and run multiple businesses, and had been an executive and a lawyer in private business and in government. I had never been part of a private legal practice. I was broke and on an eat-what-you-kill deal with the firm. In other words, I was on straight commission.

In February, I brought home a check of less than $600. This amount was for the entire month. I cried the entire half-hour drive home. That day, I vowed never to let another man control my life. I would never again put my family in the position of someone else calling our shots. I would never again let another person have so much power over my life and my whole family's financial security.

At this point, I knew what I didn't want. I didn't want my hard work to be of more value to someone else that it was to me. I knew if I wanted financial security, I had to slow down; I had to plan more, understand more, and build my business stronger—with less outside control. That was what was right for me. That was what success looked like to me when I saw the end first. That is where I decided I would take my family.

On that winter day, I did not know what would lead us to that financial success and security. Yet as I worked in that firm, I began to sense that maybe my road had taken me back home to law.

> **GOLDEN NUGGET**
>
> *I knew if I wanted financial security, I had to slow down; I had to plan more, understand more, and build my business stronger–with less outside control.*
>
>

The hard work my wife and I had done in the past, combined with the lessons we had already learned and with the hard work I would undergo over the next two years as I built the idea for my new firm, had taught me Rule One's final lesson. Ultimately, we arrived at success in a way I had not originally thought of or planned. Sometimes the road to success may take a detour, and that detour is the right road!

CHAPTER TWO

CONSISTENT COMPETENCY IS BETTER THAN ERRATIC EXCELLENCE

2

Hard work will eventually pay off

CONSISTENT COMPETENCY IS BETTER THAN ERRATIC EXCELLENCE

Never go into the ring without the will to win

No human being will work hard at anything unless they believe that they are working for competence.

—William Glasser

The end of education is to see men made whole, both in competence and in conscience.

—John Dickey

There's a lot more to competence than a law degree and a modicum of courtroom skill.

—Senator Fred Thompson

DON'T STRIVE FOR EXCELLENCE TOO SOON

I firmly believe we strive for excellence way too early in this country. As surprising as that might sound, I'm being completely serious.

We have raised a whole generation of people who think you can bypass simple competency and go straight to excellence. These people have developed the mentality that the minutiae of becoming fully competent are irrelevant, that competence is beneath our society of "excellence," and that the concept of building success by building blocks of experiences and skills upon each other does not apply.

A big part of this fallacy is our society's increasing tendency to reward everyone, no matter each individual effort or result. Everybody gets a trophy; all people are told how wonderful they are, even when they have not made the grade. Even if productivity on the plant floor is below profit levels, no one wants to say, "You haven't even mastered the basics of your job, so how do you think you deserve an 'excellent' on your review?"

It is happening everywhere. Our schools and our students lag behind many other countries in math, and many schools no longer teach the kids their multiplication tables. In contrast, I still remember mine and can quickly repeat them all the way up to the tens. That's not important, you might say, because our kids have calculators on their phones and computers. Oh yeah? Ever watched a young person from this generation try to find a percentage, add a string of numbers, or make change just by using his or her head? If you want to have some real fun, give a young cashier an odd amount of money in order to minimize the change in your pocket and watch him or her try to figure out what just happened.

Recently, a Massachusetts high school teacher gave a commencement address in which he dealt with this issue of excess reward and a lack of competency. David McCullough, of Wellesley High School, said:

We have come to love accolades more than genuine achievement...We have come to see them as the point, and we're happy to compromise standards or ignore reality if we suspect that it is the quickest way or only way to have something to put on the mantelpiece, something to pose with, crow about, [or] something with which to leverage ourselves into a better spot on the social totem pole.

In my life, competence has been required. For example, when I started my new job with the law firm, I needed to learn how to make money and I needed to learn quickly. I had no desire to go back to delivering pizzas. I wanted to strive for excellence in my career, but I needed to become competent first.

To achieve this competency, I worked long and hard hours. I would see anybody who might have a legal matter on which I could work. I spent time with the firm's staff in order to learn how work and cash flowed into the office. I quizzed other lawyers about their firms, too.

When I was assigned to take on some injury law cases involving workers' compensation, I read the statutes from front to back. I read all the cases and the books about those cases. I wanted to know how to make it in this business, and I wanted to apply the business competencies I had learned over the previous decade.

One of those business competencies I had learned was the importance of marketing and advertising. Legal marketing has a complex history. Until the early 1900s, lawyers freely advertised their businesses, just like any other consumer service or goods provider might. In fact, Abraham Lincoln advertised his law firm, Lincoln & Herndon, before he left Illinois to take the oath of office for the presidency.

However, in the early 1900s, the elites made an effort to control the legal business through three methods (there's that three again!). First, they required all lawyers attend a law school in order to restrict access to the discipline. Prior to that time, anyone could "read for the law," as Lincoln and others before him had done. This entailed an on-the-job, apprenticeship-type of training. After the training, a panel of licensed lawyers reviewed candidates before the latter could be admitted to practice.

Second, the elites required a strict adherence to a fee schedule. They accomplished this by making up a so-called ethics rule whereby they would take away your law license if you dared charge a lesser fee than prescribed.

Finally, they outlawed lawyer advertising, again by making up an ethics rule.

Over the years, state and federal courts have undone most of these restrictions in order to allow free competition. (They have maintained the restriction requiring law students to go to an accredited law school before they can sit for the bar exam.) For example, in 1977, the U.S. Supreme Court re-approved advertising by lawyers in the landmark case of *Bates v. Arizona*. Recently, several lawsuits, including class action cases, have been filed to challenge law schools that oversold the promised results of graduates passing the bar and obtaining jobs.

I hope these lawsuits are the first step in removing the last vestige of those anticompetitive rules.

When I examined the practice of law in my capacity as an entrepreneur and business executive, and as I envisioned what kind of firm I wanted to build and how I would do it, taking advantage of the free market and advertising became a critical part of the equation.

Computerization was the second competency I had learned through my experience. I knew I would gain a competitive edge from developing computer systems that could keep up with a law practice's minutiae and leave each lawyer more time to be a lawyer. I began to research management systems and advertising options.

After conducting my research, I developed a plan to grow the firm and presented my proposal to the owner. He was (and still is) a good lawyer with a good reputation. I proposed his name and face become the firm's visual brand, while I would handle the business's executive and managerial aspects.

Fortunately for me, he turned down my idea.

Yes, fortunately. His refusal meant I would have to do it myself and build my own firm.

Then, in early 1989, I had my next idea: I would bring business principles back to the practice of consumer law.

As I mentioned before, when researching my new practice I looked at the various services a law firm could provide, including real estate, bankruptcy, domestic, and injury law. I chose injury law because I have always loved the medical field.

Even though I had an affinity for medicine and had had experiences in law school most lawyers have never had, I had laid all that aside. Then, almost ten years later, after developing competency in business, I poured myself into cases that involved medicine, and developed a competency in medical law I had flirted with years earlier.

I hadn't become competent in business overnight. When I had reached for the golden ring, which is akin to striving for erratic excellence, the situation hadn't always worked out as planned, assuming I even had a plan. However, ten years of building and operating businesses had created a level of competence—consistent excellence—that would serve me well in running and growing a law firm.

HOW DO WE BECOME COMPETENT?

There are real consequences for people who try to skip the competencies and go straight to excellence. First, this mentality lulls you into a false definition of excellence, based on the zeal to give rewards constantly. Second, you must have a full understanding of the basics of your job, your project, your sport, or your marriage. If you do not, your chances of succeeding in any of those areas, when push comes to shove, are significantly reduced. If a society's core workforce loses its competencies, the result is a diminishing middle class and the associated need for expanded governmental services.

> **GOLDEN NUGGET**
>
> *If a society's core workforce loses its competencies, the result is a diminishing middle class and the associated need for expanded governmental services.*
>
>

Sound familiar?

Life hasn't always been that way. In the past, society encouraged competency through a variety of methods. Apprenticeships, for example, ensured that people entered a trade or a profession at the bottom, learned their business from the ground up, and became knowledgeable in all aspects of the tasks necessary to their jobs. Only then were they allowed to practice or to receive the title of "Master," as in Master Mechanic, Master Cobbler, or Master Electrician.

Abraham Lincoln was such an example in the professional world. He never went to law school; instead, he read for the law. As mentioned earlier, this entailed spending several years reading the law books of his day and working for a sponsoring lawyer. After spending several years gaining enough competency in the law, in its rules, and in actual day-to-day practice, Lincoln's sponsoring lawyer presented him to other lawyers and judges. These individuals questioned Lincoln to determine if he was deemed fit to practice law.

Contrast that experience with the one provided by the law schools of today, which do little to teach the core competencies of practicing law. Most students get out of law school knowing the law's technical aspects, but they don't know how to practice it, how to give their clients great service, or how to build their business without losing themselves. The result? The licensing bars across this nation have had to become business regulators. They spend more time tracking down lawyers who don't return clients' phone calls, who tell clients they did work when they didn't, or who steal money from clients, than they do regulating business in order to make sure clients receive good advice and counsel.

In all my years as a licensed lawyer, I have never seen a lawyer disbarred because he or she consistently gave crappy legal advice. However, I have seen lawyers lose licenses or be disciplined because they did not consistently and competently provide the normal, simple business services any client should expect. If only law schools spent a significant, mandatory amount of time on all aspects of practicing law, rather than focusing on the technical legal portion, licensing bars would have an easier job and the clients would be better served. If schools did that, lawyers, especially new lawyers, would be competent in their practice, not just their knowledge, of law.

In our business-focused society today, franchises play apprenticeships' former role. Studies have found that people who buy a franchise are much more likely to be successful and stay in business than people who go it alone. Why? The franchisors have already seen the end first. They know what success looks like for their business model and have determined the core competencies needed for that particular business. They have modeled it for the franchisees. They teach franchisees these core competencies and require the businesses to operate within their standard model of competencies. Sure, they allow franchisees to experiment, but they only add a new product or method into their larger model after testing for effectiveness and reliability. As with apprenticeships, during which the student learns the master's business model from the ground up, each franchisee learns the franchised model and seeks to replicate it. Because considerable thought, planning, and execution have already gone into the core competencies needed for that business to succeed, the modern-day apprentice—the franchisee—has a leg up on the success ladder.

In addition to the apprenticeship method, sometimes it takes good old basics and repetition to become consistently competent and ultimately excellent. As Baron Baptiste, noted yoga instructor and author of the book *Journey into Power,* said, "It is a simple but crucial rule that for any level of transformational success, you must develop the spirit of repetition and consistency. Repetition is the mother of skill, and skill is the mother of mastery."

Similarly, the legendary football coach Vince Lombardi understood that if we want to perform at a high level of consistent excellence, including at the professional level of achievement, we must constantly review, learn, and practice the core competencies of our sport or job.

I got my first glimpse into Vince Lombardi and his techniques from a man named Carroll Dale, a wide receiver for the Green Bay Packers. Dale, who played in Super Bowls I and II, was coached by Lombardi. When I was young, my family lived near Tri-City Airport in Tennessee. Dale, whose home was in Virginia, would often travel through the Tri-City Airport. On one of those trips, I was honored to meet him and talk to him, courtesy of an introduction by my dad, who worked for Piedmont Airlines.

One thing Dale told me was how Lombardi would always open training camp with words that have now become famous. Lombardi would stand up in front of these professionals, hold up a football, and say, "Gentlemen, this is a football." He would explain what a football was, why it was shaped the way it was, and what role it played in the game. After that, they would go outside and he would explain the field, the out-of-bounds lines, the yard lines, and why all those lines were important. He would explain the elementary aspects of running, tackling, and passing. He knew that if he wanted to have an excellent, champion-level football team, then that team must be consistently competent in *all* aspects of the game and of their individual jobs.

When was the last time you explained to your employees, or even to your kids, the basics of what to do, why those basics are important, and how they fit into the model of success you envision?

I don't remember every word Dale told me when I was eleven years old. However, I do remember he told me to work hard, practice everything related to the sport, and always play to win. Even then, I was being fed the seeds of the Three Rules. I understood them as much as a kid my age could, and I have never forgotten them.

Other words from my youth, which remain with me more than any others, are these: "Give me a bingle, a base single, give me a bingle!"

My dad spoke these words countless times to all the players, including me, who were on his Little League teams. Dad believed in consistent core competencies so much that on his teams you weren't allowed to swing for the fences (that is, to get a home run). He just wanted each player to get on base, get a single hit, and load up the bases. He knew that if every player on our team had a goal of just getting on base—don't swing for the fences or try to "hot dog" it, he'd encourage, just get a single and get on base—we would score more runs and win more games. He was right. We fielded balls, threw them correctly, and practiced running bases in all the situations that might come up. We never took those mighty swings for the fences you see so often in Little League games.

As a result, our team members got on base a lot. We won a lot. When I was thirteen, my family moved from Tennessee to North Carolina. Dad brought those same skills to a group of unwanted extra kids, including the first girl in the league. One "bingle" at a time, he turned them into a winning team. Dad understood what Dale understood and what Lombardi understood, too. You can only hope to be consistently competent if you first become competent in all of your game's aspects. You can only become consistently excellent if you become consistently competent.

In the business world, McDonald's is a company that understands consistent competence is better than erratic excellence. I have never seen or heard that McDonald's corporate vision is to give customers the best hamburger, the best-designed restaurant, or the best dining experience in the world. No. What McDonald's wants is for a customer to be driving down the road and say, "I'm hungry. There's probably a Mickie D's at the next exit, and the burger will taste the same there, the fries will be cooked the same there, and the bathroom will be located in about the same place there as in the one back home. It may not be the best meal of the day, but I know exactly what I'm getting."

McDonald's executives want their restaurants to be consistently competent, which is a tough job when a company has thousands of stores and hundreds of thousands of employees. Yet they are successful in giving customers a consistently competent product and experience.

When I went to work in that law firm, back in 1988, I saw how many lawyers were great technical lawyers. They understood the legal aspects of their practice, but they were not consistently competent in all aspects of running their businesses. That, I surmised, would be my competitive advantage, my "unique selling proposition," and my "secret sauce."

In the midsummer of 1989, I made a fateful decision. On my way home from work, I decided to let my wife in on my desire to start my own firm.

As you might imagine, that was not a pleasant experience. I fully understand why. We were just getting back on our feet. Bill Boyd had helped us get a small house with sweat equity. Teresa and I had done the insulating and painting, and my brother-in-law, a licensed electrician, had done the electrical. (As a matter of fact, Robb, my friend and editor, and his wife Linda spent several weekends helping us paint so we could get out of our apartment and into the house.)

I was busy with about ninety clients and was bringing home consistent paychecks each month. You can see why Teresa would not have been enamored with the idea of chucking my job and starting our own firm. After all, we had been homeless and living with Teresa's parents less than two years earlier.

However, I had been doing the research. I had a strong plan of how to attack the market based on the business principles I had learned and through advertising and computerization. Once I promised I would not have partners who could pull our plug, and that the deal would be dependent upon me, Teresa agreed. We began to make plans to start our own company again.

We launched our own law firm in October 1989. Our credit still wasn't great, so both sets of our parents had to guarantee a $3,500 bank loan. Okay, so our credit was lousy. Yet we started our firm with that loan. My first purchase was a computer and management software. We didn't have fancy desks or chairs, but we did have the latest and greatest computer systems to help us grow.

And grow we did. My wife and I started with just one other person: a secretary who came over from the other firm. Within six months, we hired a second staff person; six months after that, we added another lawyer. We had ups and downs, and our cash flow was tight, but we dreamed of being a big firm.

I took advantage of the renewed right for lawyers to advertise. I was the first lawyer in the city of Asheboro, North Carolina, to take something more than a professional announcement ad in the phone book. I took a whole page and then the whole back cover.

To say most of my fellow lawyers in town disapproved would be a huge understatement. I had decided to become the visual brand of our law firm. I would be the brand's face, not necessarily a pretty one, but the face. I put my face front and center in the ads because I wanted people to see a human face when they thought of my firm. In our offices, we did not use the normal, law-firm décor of plush leather chairs with fancy British hunt club pictures on the wall. Instead, my wife picked out soothing colors in teal, gray, and purple. She selected comforting and inviting pictures for the walls. Our research had shown that women made the majority of purchasing decisions when their families hired lawyers, and so we wanted our firm to be an inviting place for them, a place where they could find refuge and not feel intimidated.

We held an open house at our firm and invited the community. That was a huge mistake! The other lawyers saw that we were setting ourselves apart with our advertising and by how we had designed our office, and they disapproved.

On one occasion, one of my competitors cut my photo out of the phonebook, drew a Hitler mustache on it, and posted it on the bulletin board of the lawyers' lounge at the courthouse. Another parodied my firm's ads in his annual Christmas Party invitations for years.

It was tough not being approved by my local peers, but I had to remind myself that my goal was for my family. I would not let the local bar's disapproval slow me down. In fact, I owe those local peers a big debt of gratitude. Because of their actions, I remained steely in my resolve and even more focused to make my success happen.

As I learned, you can listen to the naysayers in your life and succumb to their negative opinions about you and your chances, or you can use that negativity as motivation. Their negativity shows you the path you do not want to take, while their jealousy is an indication of what you never want to become.

By 1992, Teresa and I were getting back on our feet. We had been in our small house for about two years when Bill Boyd said to us, "You need a bigger house, one with a bedroom for each of your girls."

Bill was a homebuilder, and it just so happened he had such a house, one he had built about a year before. It was just the right size for us: three bedrooms, was on a single level, and was less than three thousand square feet. We loved it, but we still had to undergo the credit test.

We passed.

Our family moved into that house, and Teresa and I still live there. My income today is more than ten times what it was in 1992, but we live in the same house. I recommend you read the book *The Millionaire Next Door*, by Thomas J. Stanley and William D. Danko; by doing so, you will see the value in our decision.

USE GOALS AND PLANS TO FIND THE COMPETENCIES YOU NEED

Let's revisit Rule One and the hard work of setting goals. Teresa and I had set a goal of starting our own law firm. However, by 1994, I realized I was still not clearly focused on my long-term goals. Teresa and I had ideas about what we wanted (to be financially sound and successful again) and what we didn't want (to be homeless and deliver pizzas again), but I had not set concrete goals with timetables.

To do so, I detailed our family business plan mentioned in this book's introduction. While the concept of three, as discussed in the introduction, had not risen to the top of my mind, I built a plan that had three parts.

Remember, we were still a small company. Teresa and I had only three employees. We were making a reasonable income, but nothing more. Jamie, my youngest child, had just finished the second grade. That's when I developed these goals.

By the time Jamie graduated from high school, Teresa and I would achieve three milestones:

1. The firm would be worth $5 million.
2. We would own $5 million in real estate holdings.
3. We would have $1 million in stocks and securities.

This timeframe gave us about ten years to achieve these goals.

That was the plan. These numbers had no magic to them and no scientific backing. They were just nice, round numbers. If Teresa and I accomplished those goals, our family's financial footing would be solid. Shoot for the moon, I had been told, so I decided to do so. As Donald Trump says, "You have to think anyway, so why not think big?"

At the time, we had no real estate apart from our house. We had no savings account, let alone any stocks and securities. Our firm was worth nothing if I wasn't in there working.

When I showed the plan to Teresa, she said, "You must be crazy."

When I told her I was going to present that plan to the bank and explain this was where we were going and we wanted the bank to grow along with us, she said, "Now, I know you're crazy!"

Crazy or not, that's exactly what I did.

I had dreamed of building a bigger firm. However, dreams are just that—dreams—until you put them down in writing, make them measurable (using times, dates, and amounts), and then share them with others. Once you do these three things, your dreams become goals.

You can accomplish goals. Accomplishing goals helps you reach your dreams. I knew that. I had learned it many times and had seen it in everything I read. Yet I had never done it to the extent I was doing it now. Now, I decided, things would be different.

Thus, I wrote my goals down, plugged in specific amounts and dates, and shared them with people. I wanted people to hold me accountable to these specifics. I did not have a detailed plan for reaching each of the three goals, but those goals were set. I had never owned any commercial real estate and didn't know where to start. I knew what stocks and bonds were, but I'd never had money to invest. In short, I didn't know how to get to the goals I had set. I only knew that if I could achieve them, my family would be financially secure.

That is how all journeys to goals must start. If we wait until we know the full measure of how to achieve those goals, we will never get started. I didn't have to know all the steps on how to achieve my goals; I just needed to set the goals, dedicate myself to figuring out how to reach them, and then do it.

After your goals are set and you have been able to see the end first, you can begin to determine all of the competencies you need to achieve those goals. When President Kennedy set the goal for our country to land a man on the moon, most of the technology necessary to do it had not even been developed. However, once the goal had been set, scientists could determine how to achieve it and then make it happen.

Once my three goals listed above were set, Teresa and I were ready to march toward them. Clearly, the firm was the first place to start. We had to build a business that would provide the income and cash flow needed to feed our other two goals. We had to understand and build the competencies necessary to become excellent.

As we advertised our firm in the Yellow Pages and then on the back cover of the phone book, our little company began to grow. From 1989 to 1993, before I had even developed my firm list of three goals, our firm moved twice, transitioning from our original four hundred square feet into three thousand square feet.

Teresa and I kept progressing toward our first goal. We met with Steve Defoe, who had developed what he called the "case-management method." This method stripped away all the non-lawyer work from the lawyer, which allowed the staff members to flourish and maximized the lawyer's time. In the early years, the case-management method and our computer system were our secret weapons.

We continued building our firm. We put in systems and processes that made us consistent. We trained, trained, and trained to become competent in technical laws, customer experience, customer service, and customer expectations. We had rules about how to return phone calls, enter client notes in our computerized client-management system, and work the checklist of tasks every single day with consistency. We instituted pay systems that took into consideration clients' ratings of our employees. We wanted to be consistently competent. If we were, we thought, we would beat our competition hands down.

We did!

The firm grew at rates unheard of in our region. Less than five years after we started advertising, we became the largest firm in our market area, even though other firms had been marketing for many years before we began doing so. This achievement culminated in us being recognized with an award from the *Triad Business Journal* for being one of the Fifty Fastest-Growing Companies of *all* companies in central North Carolina.

Our consistent competency gained us a positive reputation with our clients and with doctors, judges, and other individuals positioned to give us good recommendations.

IDENTIFY THE NECESSARY CORE COMPETENCIES AND MASTER THEM

Determining the core competencies you need in whatever endeavor you undertake is a critical part of your ultimate success. Remember, though, you have to see the end first and have a vision for where you are going. If you don't, how will you ever identify and develop the core competencies you need? If you know where you are going, then identify the necessary core competencies, ensure you can achieve them, and work to attain them consistently. You will have a better chance of achieving what you really strive for: consistent excellence.

The problem with striving for excellence too soon is that it is not sustainable.

"Oh, Bob," you might be thinking, "that's heresy. We should always seek excellence."

Nope. That would be wrong. First, we should strive for competency. For excellence to shine through that competency, a whole series of events must line up. A host of factors go into excellence, whether we seek that excellence in the job we do, a concert we attend, or a meal we eat. Most of those factors are outside our control. That area of non-control is where the fan starts turning the fastest when the smelly stuff hits. When we are not fully competent in all of the factors of our job, we minimize the window of excellence available to us. In contrast, when we master our core competencies, and live and work within them consistently, we open that window wide.

Think about it this way. As the CEO of your small business, you should be competent in the three basic parts of running a business. These include:

1. operations, the actual doing of what you do;
2. finance and accounting; and
3. marketing, advertising, and sales.

Bigger operations may include other major functions, but these are the basic three. What a coincidence: here's the power of three at work again.

As a CEO, if you are competent in all of those areas, you and your company will be on more stable ground. If you have a hiccup in operations, for example, your finance acumen can kick in with creative ways to solve your cash crunch, while your accounting competency will allow you to have the necessary financial documents any

GOLDEN NUGGET

By being competent in all aspects of your business, you broaden your view and throw that window for success wide open.

banker or investor would want. By being competent in all aspects of your business, you broaden your view and throw that window for success wide open.

Let's face it; nobody is excellent all the time. Nowhere is this fact more glaring than in the sport of golf.

I am not a golfer, but I like to see golf when it comes to town. Several years back, I was at a tournament in Greensboro, North Carolina, watching Fred Couples. Couples is a great golfer, a champion. However, on the fourth hole, he hit his ball down an embankment on the right side of the fairway. The ball almost went into a little pond.

I don't know what caused that less than excellent shot. Maybe there was a gust of wind. Maybe Couples moved a millimeter off in his swing at that critical moment. Whatever the cause, his ball lay at the bottom of the embankment, inches from the water.

Couples calmly walked to the ball and looked down at it with an expression on his face that said, "Been here before." He took out a club, put his left foot on top of the embankment and his right foot almost in the water, and calmly hit a shot that landed his ball about three feet from the cup.

"That was the same guy," I thought. "The same guy who nearly put it in the water almost put it in the hole."

How? Why? Couples came back from this obstacle because he is a consistently competent golfer. I didn't say he was competent all the time, and I didn't say he was excellent every time. Instead, he is consistently competent. He was familiar with the situation and knew how to overcome it. As he faced that precarious position, he had a big window of opportunity because of his competency in all aspects of his game.

This example shows that consistent competency gives you a solid base from which to perform. It widens your opportunity for success. When things do go wrong, you have a better platform from which to launch your second shot.

Erratic excellence, in contrast, can be fun sometimes. However, it is not, by its definition, sustainable. We can all remember that game we played or that fantastic day at work in which we had one shining moment when we performed in a way that surprised even us. We were excellent. We can still feel it and we have told everybody we know about it at least once. That moment stands out so much because it was, and is, a rarity.

GOLDEN NUGGET

Do you want to be a one-hit wonder or do you want to have an entire career's worth of hits?

Do you want a life of rare and erratic excellence, or do you want to stack the deck in your favor and try to have more of those excellent days? Do you want to be a one-hit wonder or do you want to have an entire career's worth of hits?

Let me be clear. I am not saying erratic excellence is bad. It's not. It's cool and fun to have those surprisingly excellent days. However, if you strive for excellence before you become consistently competent, you minimize your long-term chances for sustainable success. True success is so hard to achieve that you need to stack the deck in your favor as much as you can.

When you are consistently competent in all aspects of your endeavors, you will be amazed by how many chances at excellence come your way. The thing is, those chances were there all along. Yet would you have recognized them or even seen them? Would they have blown past you because you hadn't opened yourself up to consistent competency?

I have never taken a course in business, marketing, advertising, or accounting. When I first started in business, I just did it using good old trial and error. I made lots of mistakes. Eventually, my brain kicked in and said, "This is nuts."

I began to educate myself about accounting, finance, and corporate structure. I even read books and corporate annual reports. You can stop laughing now. Yes, I am that guy who actually reads those things, and they have taught me a lot.

By 1994, Teresa and I were ready to take that next big step for our firm and advertise on television. I had met some lawyers from Kentucky while at a conference, and they introduced me to the folks at their ad agency, which was based in Nashville, Tennessee. Two guys started the ad agency, which specialized in law firms: Arnie Malham provided the vision and analysis, while Emmy Award-winning Jimmy Bewley provided the creativity.

Arnie, the CEO, had developed a sophisticated method of tracking every incoming phone call to a client's office and correlating it with the client's TV ads to measure each ad's performance. This allowed the firm's clients to achieve maximum results with a minimum budget.

Maximum results with minimum budget? This sounded just like what the doctor ordered for our firm.

Off we went to Nashville to shoot our first commercials. Because I was still the face of the firm, I acted as the "on-air talent." Our firm could handle the advertising expense, but just barely. We started with a budget of just $1,000 per week, and we were scared to death. I know this amount doesn't seem like a lot, but back in 1994, when we had only one office and a small staff, it was a huge commitment.

I met with our employees and told them the firm was going on TV. After I told them how much it would cost, I assured them they would be paid first, the ad agency second, other bills third, and our family last, if there was any money left over.

Many months, Teresa and I took our house payment to the bank just before 2:00 p.m. on the last day it was due. We didn't take regular paychecks; we just drew the bare minimum to survive. We reinvested everything we had in the firm. We were all in. Our plan was to become a large injury-law firm.

Arnie and Jimmy filled in the blanks for me. While Teresa and I were building our brand through our high level of service, they were teaching me how to maximize that brand with advertising and marketing, how to work on camera, and how to spend a lot less than my competitors while getting more cases.

A few years later, I faced a dilemma. I wanted the law firm to grow into a new TV market. I also wanted to allow some younger lawyers to buy in to the firm, but didn't know how to structure the buy-in. After all, a law firm couldn't franchise.

Then I had an idea. What if I operated my business like a franchise and structured the law firm more like a modern corporation, rather than a traditional law firm? That is what I did. We set up a second law firm, licensed the primary firm's name to the new firm, and allowed the younger lawyers to invest in the company.

According to Lloyd's of London, we were the first law firm in the U.S. to operate that way. Why was Lloyd's of London involved? Our malpractice insurance carrier had never seen this type of structure in a law firm before, so its representatives had to go to their re-insurer, Lloyd's of London, to get approval to write our coverage.

The second company we set up did very well. Just a few years ago, the other lawyers we hired relied on that success to purchase a significant portion of our primary firm.

No, I am not a finance and accounting expert. However, had I not become competent in these areas through years of reading and applying myself, then it's likely I would not have seen this great growth opportunity and I might have missed it. Instead, I had mastered all the competencies I needed, including television advertising, marketing, finance, and customer service at levels unheard of in law firms (such as calling clients at 9:30 p.m. to let them know we were still on the case).

Ultimately, we made an excellent decision that has paid off beautifully for me and for the lawyers who made those initial investments.

COMPETENCY AND EXCELLENCE
ARE MOVING TARGETS

In your job, as an entrepreneur, and even as a spouse or parent, what are the core competencies necessary for success? You must continually ask yourself that question because excellence is an ever-moving target.

When I first started in business, Al Gore had not yet invented the Internet. Do you think you can be a competent CEO today without having a competent working knowledge of the Internet or knowing how to market and position your company? You don't have to be an Internet maven or nerd, but you had better understand the web's potential and process, and know how to integrate its usage into your business at every level.

Today, the twice-monthly payroll, just for our law firm, dwarfs the entire amount of money we grossed our first two years in business. Like every other developer in this country, my real estate company has experienced excessive vacancies, a difficult banking environment, and delayed or canceled projects. There is no way I could have anticipated all of the business issues we now face. However, I prepared as best I could by developing a core set of competencies, a basis from which the company can build and a foundation upon which the company can stand.

Competency is not something we achieve one fine day and grow no more. Competency is an ever-evolving thing; because of that, it requires your attention and active examination.

Recently, I befriended a younger executive who, because of family issues, will be at a holding point in his career for the next three to five years. He chooses to be at this holding point and honors it. However, he wants to be ready for the next step in his career when the time is right.

The advice I gave to him is the same as the advice I give to you. Conduct a very detailed and honest assessment of where you are now compared to the job or position you want or the goal you want to attain. Contact old bosses or co-workers who will be honest with you and let them weigh in on your strengths and weaknesses. If you haven't taken assessments relating your personality to different job types, consider undergoing those as well. Measure your core competencies against those of your competitors and see where you are lacking. At that point, begin developing your plan to gain those competencies.

I'm amazed by how many folks never do that. As I discussed in Chapter One, many folks never sit down and decide what it is they really want, either. However, isn't this what a coach does for players? A coach assesses a player's strengths and weaknesses, sees what can be improved, and then sets on a course to improve it.

This process starts with seeing the end result you want first and then conducting an assessment of where you are in relation to that result.

I have taken one of those assessments. I will never forget that terrible day or the incredibly positive impact it had on me. This assessment took place when I worked for David Stedman's company. In that company, each management person had to take a battery of personality tests and attend a five-day executive development workshop. I was sure I didn't need to do this because, you see, I was an ideas guy and a hard worker. I thought I was it. I had not yet been a pizza pusher, which may give you a clue about my problem: a lack of humility. I took the tests and went to the workshop. About an hour into my first day, I had not said a word. Then, the moderator turned straight to me and said, "You think this is a lot of shit, don't you?" (That is a direct quotation.)

I said, "Well, I wouldn't use that word, but that about sums it up."

The moderator picked up my file, quickly looked at a couple of papers, and said, "Let's see, your personality is best described as a 'let's party' type. Your brain works very fast, so you know the answer before most people have time to digest the question. When you add that capacity to your 'let's party' personality, the result is you often blurt out the answer or overwhelm others in the room with your analysis. This happens so much so that they often think you are an ass! Yeah, that about covers it, doesn't it?"

I was stunned. The people I had met just an hour before, who were also attending the session, were stunned. While I was that moderator's first victim that day, I was by no means his last. Fortunately, instead of hurting me, his words have helped me. Many times since then, I have repeated his words to myself and worked to keep my mouth shut. Sometimes this method works; sometimes the beast inside me gets out. However, working on this has helped me get to know my inner self. Overall, the moderator's willingness that day to approach me with the truth has helped me immensely.

As you read this book, I hope you examine yourself relative to your job or your family, and ask yourself these questions:

- Am I competent in all aspects of my endeavors?
- Am I competent enough to be consistently competent?
- If not, where are my weaknesses? What can I do about them?

I hope you will give yourself the gift of examination. I'm not asking you to wallow in your limitations. Instead, I'm encouraging you to glimpse who you really are, learn what your strengths are, and discover how to play to those strengths.

As you become consistently competent in all aspects of your endeavors, you will find your ability to weather the ups and downs becomes greater. The windows of opportunity will open more widely, and you will have more moments of true excellence.

To achieve the end you saw first, rely on your consistent competencies. Performing them consistently and competently will lead you to the ultimate goal of consistent excellence and success.

CHAPTER THREE

NEVER GO INTO THE RING WITHOUT THE WILL TO WIN

3

Hard work will eventually pay off

Consistent competency is better than erratic excellence

NEVER GO INTO THE RING WITHOUT THE WILL TO WIN

RINGS AS SYMBOLS

Think back to my description of that first day, when I said these rules for the first time. It was a hot summer day at a smelly horse show. Brandi had just ridden a not-so-pretty event, and our conversation about the rules and why she felt so bad about her performance followed. Because she had just exited the riding ring, it was appropriate that Rule Three included the word *ring*.

The more I reflected on my rules and the words I had said, the more I realized how all-encompassing the word *ring* was on that day and is for all of us today.

You see, our society attaches a tremendous symbolism to rings:

- We seal our hearts and our feelings with rings when we commit to friendships, promises, engagements, and weddings.
- A politician "throws his hat into the ring" when he announces his candidacy for public office.
- The Romans built coliseums in circles, or rings, just as we build sports stadiums, arenas, and NASCAR tracks today.

- Athletes worldwide gather every four years under a banner of five rings to participate in the Olympic Games.
- Rings are a popular symbol in movies and music. Johnny Cash sang about "The Ring of Fire" and *The Lion King* referred to "The Circle of Life."

Each ring symbolizes something unique, yet all rings have the same qualities. A ring has no beginning or end. Each ring encompasses the whole of the experience it represents. Whether you step into a ring or put one on your finger, you know that ring-related moment is of singular import.

> **GOLDEN NUGGET**
>
> *A ring has no beginning or end. Each ring encompasses the whole of the experience it represents.*
>
>

Having the concept of a *ring* in the final rule emphasizes that whenever we are working on any worthwhile endeavor, be it achieving financial independence, winning a horse show, or committing our lives to someone else, we are experiencing a special moment. Since we are engaged in an important process, we should value it as we would value a ring.

FOCUSING ON WHY

What is this rule of rings about?

The first two rules discussed in this book help you determine *what* success means for you in terms of hard work (Rule One) and *how* to achieve that success through consistent competency (Rule Two).

Rule Three helps you determine *why* you will succeed; it helps you discover the will to win. This rule is about finding your attitude and passion, and then giving yourself the best opportunity to succeed.

Determining your Rule Three reason is critical to your success. This *why* is your passion and driving force. It is that thing inside you motivating you to do the hard work you signed up for when you evaluated Rules One and Two. Of the Three Rules, this one is the most personal. (Some might say it's the most important, although I wouldn't.)

"But, Bob," you might be wondering, "how can it be more personal than deciding what it is you want in Rule One?"

I have two reasons to explain why your interpretation of Rule Three is most personal. First, your will to win is what fires you, what gives you passion, and drives what you want. Second, this will to win (or passion, attitude, or whatever else you want to call it) will push you further through the tough times, lift you up over the devastating times, and give you that singular moment of satisfaction when that end, which you saw first, is finally actualized.

At our law firm, this passion is directed to our clients. I have always had an abiding love and passion for underdogs. Most of our clients are underdogs who have no voice in society and no real power; the playing field is not tilted their way—until we come along. We stand up for them, level that playing field, and force the powerful to be accountable. Frequently, at our company, we say, "Take care of the client, and the money will take care of itself." That is our truth and we live it. Battles against powerful, moneyed interests would be too hard, and the fight year in and year out would be too long, if we did not have a passion for assisting injured people.

If you are in an organization or a company, it would be ideal if you shared that organization's passion. However, you do not have to come to that passion from the same place.

For instance, I developed my passion for helping injured folks because of my experience growing up poor and seeing the difference power and money made. In contrast, Chris Roberts, who is now our law firm's CEO, came to his passion from a different path. He was involved in a serious accident and experienced firsthand the difficulties life thrusts upon you when you are injured. While the origins of our passion to aid the injured are different, our power, intent, and commitment are the same.

Most successful endeavors are similar. Success is difficult. That concept is so important, it's part of this book's title. I don't care if you are working to become a chess champion, a successful business owner, or a successful spouse and/or parent. Because success is tough, if you don't have a passion for what you attempt, you will not have anywhere near the amount of strength required to see the process through. In times of trouble, you will grow weary past the point of return, or you will turn to your lesser self, the one in which anger and bitterness reside.

> **GOLDEN NUGGET**
> *Because success is tough, if you don't have a passion for what you attempt, you will not have anywhere near the amount of strength required to see the process through.*

Passion does not make the journey to success easier. It does not smooth out the road so it is all easy going. However, passion will smooth you out. Passion will help you refocus and rebuild. It will give you strength when you need that strength. Sometimes, it will give you just enough of the gut-check desire not to let failure grasp you. Passion will keep you in the ring with the will to win.

HAVE MULTIPLE PASSIONS AND AMBITIONS

There are a lot of wills to win in my life. I work hard and take chances in business because I want to be financially secure, both for my family and for myself. I work hard at understanding and being there for my kids because they need me; after all, I need them too. I take chances in life, like flying airplanes, writing songs, and racing cars, because I don't want to be on my deathbed saying, "I wish I'd..."

I challenge you to live your life with positive excitement and passion as well. Apply this Rule Three philosophy—going into the ring with the will to win—in every aspect of your life.

For instance, two of my employees and friends, Marshall Hurley and Phil Young, have taken up photography with a passion. I am excited to see them build that part of their lives into something that holds value and joy. During the time in which they've been working on their passion, neither has missed a single opportunity or work obligation at our company. Instead, the developing passion they have for photography has carried over into their work, their focus (sorry about that pun), and their attitude. That possibility for extension is one of the great things about passion and attitude. When passion is up in one area, it bleeds over to other areas. Likewise, when that dark cloud of negativity permeates one area of your life, it can't help but spill over and infect other areas of your life.

The important thing, then, is to identify the wills to win and passions in your life—and they need to be *yours*. They shouldn't be mine, your parents', or even your spouse's. (Of course, if you want a happy and long marriage, pleasing your spouse had better be one of your interests.) Later on in this chapter, I will share some pointers about how to find your reason why and how to keep the will to win in the moment. Prior to that, I want to share with you some of the limiting factors we use on ourselves.

FEAR OR EXCITEMENT?

Passion and attitude can be driven by joy, fear, excitement, or dread. Any extreme can be a foolhardy, bad place to start from, but including a little of each in your attitude is a good thing.

I love building things and starting new ventures, as you have probably already guessed. I loved this side of entrepreneurialism so much that in the past I would work too hard too soon, often busting forth, headfirst, into something new without first setting a specific, measurable goal other than a general idea of "success." Typically, I was so intent on my undefined success that I did not always understand the risks or the processes a particular venture needed. For a long time, I chased erratic excellence before I had gained consistent competency. I too often learned the hard way that I gained experience right after I needed it.

Yes, I had—and still have—a passion for building something new. When I set out to build our family's three-point business plan, I was excited about it. However, my fear of being homeless again, after our big failure in 1987, truly tempered my exhilaration regarding a new venture with facing the reality of clearly defined goals and accountability systems. I also developed a maturity about financial success I did not have before. Finally, I figured out that if I continued to push headlong into new projects without making detailed and achievable plans, or without developing the competencies to complete those plans, I was destined to repeat failure.

A little fear can be good thing. However, I am not talking about a massive fear of failure. Everyone has some fear of failure, but if that fear is the primary motivating force in your life, your likelihood of achieving success will greatly diminish. You will start more slowly, you will find excuses to procrastinate, you will self-sabotage, and, deep inside, you will be happy when the forces of the universe line up against you. You will meet your expectations of failure.

Yoga instructor Baron Baptiste puts it this way: "Believing your doubts is one of the most insidious mind tricks that your ego can play on you. Doubts are not real; they are just illusions created to keep ourselves from taking risks because we are so afraid of failing."

My yoga instructor, Patricia Finegan Hunter, adds, "Fear, being just a word, carries only the weight you give it...Give fear no substance...Carry your own weight!"

When I say it's good to have a little fear, I don't mean self-limiting or paralyzing fear. Instead, I mean the fear that causes appropriate caution. In yoga, we do these poses called *shoulder stands*. In a shoulder stand, you start on your back and then strive to lift your body into the air. You keep your weight on your shoulders, your torso and legs high in the air, and your head in neutral center on the mat. Both Baron and Patricia say not to move your head from side to side in this pose. If you do, they say, you can put too much strain on your neck and hurt yourself. They do not tell us this to cause so much fear that we don't even try the pose; instead, they do so to create in us the respect the pose deserves.

The same principle applied to me and to my joy in starting new things. I needed an appropriate level of fear to join with my overabundance of joy. This mixture would slow me down, help me respect my situation, and help me plan my business ventures more completely and realistically.

While too many people have a fear of failure that keeps them from committing to a venture, failure can be a good thing. We should not go into any venture expecting it to fail, nor should we stop moving forward because we are paralyzed with fear. Sometimes, despite all of our best efforts, we fail in our ultimate goal. If so, embrace that failure!

Our greatest lessons can come from failure. Bill Gates once stated he wished his employees would have a great failure early on. Most of us have heard the saying, "You learn more from your mistakes than from your successes." Early success—heck, even later success—can be an alluring thing that throws normally level-headed people off their center and leads them to make foolish decisions. I gave myself plenty of failures to learn by because I was so bound and determined to be successful and because I was so overconfident in my abilities.

History is replete with people who learned from their mistakes and failures, believed in themselves, and went on to tremendous success. History is also littered with people who failed early on, maybe as early as high school, and determined their lives were ruined, over, and always destined to be less than what they had hoped.

Both of these groups of people were correct.

An extreme fear of failure will bind you up. It can either cause you to be inactive or overactive in an out-of-balance way. However, the desire to avoid something bad, along with a healthy dose of the desire to make something better, can be excellent motivation.

DON'T LET FEAR ROB YOU OF THE START

Often people fear failure so much that they don't even try. Sometimes they worry about not making the mark or about what others will say if they do not make the mark. A big part of this worry is because they do not see the full task road laid out before them in the beginning. They don't know how they will make their dream come true, so they don't even start. I said this earlier, but the concept bears repeating. When you set goals, you do not need to know the entire road you must travel to achieve each goal. You must see the end and envision what that end looks like, but you do not need to know—heck, there's no way you can know—all of the twists and turns, detours, and roadblocks you will likely face. If you know the entire road ahead of time, perhaps your goal is not big enough.

When I speak with people about setting goals and moving forward, I can always count on someone saying, "I wouldn't even know where to start."

This reaction is usually grounded in fear, the kind of fear that can kill dreams and goals. Don't worry about the road. Don't worry about how to do it in the beginning; just start by seeing the end first! First, you should start with a dream. Second, you should make that dream into a goal by setting

> **GOLDEN NUGGET**
> *You must be ready to make constant adjustments, change your tactics, and bob and weave as your path throws you curves.*
>
>

targets, timelines, and accountability systems. Third, you should begin to determine the first steps in making that goal a reality and the success of that dream becomes likelihood. Then, you must be ready to make constant adjustments, change your tactics, and bob and weave as your path throws you curves.

Use the rules in this book to *achieve the rules in this book.* To calm your fears, look at your end goal and try to figure out what competencies you will need in order to meet this goal. Write the competencies down, measure yourself against them, and take the time to fill in your gaps. Just embarking on this simple process of seeing the end first and examining the consistent competencies you need can give you enough faith and strength to overcome your fear and just start.

Remember, this process is like eating an elephant: you've got to do it one bite at a time. Decide if you are going to start at the head or the tail, and start eating.

Let's go back to the concept of a healthy amount of fear. When I mention discovering a motivating fear, I'm thinking of a healthy level of concern that points you in the right direction, as long as that concern does not overtake you and become your master.

I want to illustrate this point with a personal example. I had been poor as a child, but my family was close. My parents were involved in their children's lives, but they were not overbearing. They told us we could succeed and be anything we wanted if we worked hard for it. Yet being poor created a kind of disconnect in my mind. I heard their message, but I was not confident I could achieve financial success. It was as if the concept of *success*, to me, did not include financial success. Still, as an adult I dreamed about this success, created goals in relation to it, and determined it would be mine.

Yet determination without action is of no value. I had a goal to attain financial success. I had even set down a firm milestone, in that family business plan, of having $1 million in stocks and securities by the time Jamie graduated from high school. However, our family had no money in the bank. I had the right attitude and the right goal, but I couldn't bring myself to put that first check in the bank. I was living out what I had learned as a child: there is always too much month at the end of the money.

GOLDEN NUGGET

Determination without action is of no value.

I am not a parent-blamer, and my discovery regarding this subject took place way before I read the book *Rich Dad, Poor Dad*, but we all incorporate how we were raised into our personalities. In my case, I was determined to break that financial cycle. I remember, vividly, the day I sent my first check off to a mutual fund, thereby beginning the stocks-and-securities leg of our family's three-legged financial success plan. It felt like a huge amount! I almost couldn't breathe as I wrote out a check for $200. That's right, $200. I still remember my fear as I put that check in the envelope: my fear about whether I could really do this, whether I could one day have more money than month, and whether I could really achieve what I had not been taught to achieve.

I bet you've also had one of these little fear issues in your life. To others, this fear might seem somewhat silly, but it's still the basis for all that holds you back. It is okay to have these fears. Just don't reside in them. Don't resign yourself to their timidity. Don't relegate yourself or your family to their borders of mediocrity.

BALANCE YOUR PASSIONS

If we are too fearful of failure, we can also go overboard in working to become successful. We can become workaholics or "successaholics." To be truly successful requires balance. People need to play, not just work. We need to build up those around us and not just focus on our own personal success.

There's a great scene in the movie *Pretty Woman* that illustrates this point. Early on in the film, the heroine Vivian, played by Julia Roberts, takes the shoes and socks off

> **GOLDEN NUGGET**
> *If we are too fearful of failure, we can also go overboard in working to become successful. We can become workaholics or "successaholics." To be truly successful requires balance.*

Edward, the hard-charging, success-at-any-cost character played by Richard Gere. Edward is uncomfortable just trying to relax in the park, and he becomes even more so when she puts his bare feet in the grass. Later in the movie, when he faces a life-changing decision, Edward finds himself in the park again. This time, he's alone. In a moment of contemplation, he takes off his shoes and walks barefoot in the grass. He realizes he had become a successaholic, someone bent on the bad part of success. It took a pretty woman to show him his humanity and to help him understand how to find a balance in his life.

Even though I set goals and worked hard to have financial success, I also wanted to be a good dad to my kids, like my father was to me. This parenting passion competed with my passion for financial success. As a result, I went to the girls' school plays. I took Jamie to her football tryouts (she was the first girl in our town to try out for the team). I was there when Brandi got those ribbons at horse shows. In our lives, Teresa and I have tried hard to achieve a balance, one that embodies true success. While I believe each individual should follow his or her vision and dreams, a self-centered, self-focused approach is not a good road to success. It's not even a decent path.

In one of our training videos created for our firm, I tell the incoming lawyers that if they become the most successful and richest lawyers, but their kids do not know them, then they will have failed. I want you to focus on and commit to your success, but in the process, do not lose the human side of yourself or the important people in your life.

HELP YOUR PEOPLE FIND THEIR PASSION

In our law firm, we had two secret weapons for growth: case management and computerization. They really weren't that secret, just underutilized in our market. Still, because they were underutilized, our use of them gave us a competitive edge. The final weapon in our arsenal, employee training and development, would prove to be the key to our meteoric growth.

From my experience in human resources and management, I knew that a company is significantly less likely to succeed in a people-focused business without good employees who believed in the organization's goals and plans, and without the necessary training. Bob Warren, my mentor and former boss back at Stedman, once told me there are only three reasons (there we go with the important number three again) people fail on a job, and two of them are the boss's fault:

1. The employees can't do the job. That's the boss's fault for hiring the wrong person.
2. They are not trained to do the job. That means the boss failed in his duty to train them.
3. They don't want to do the job. If the boss has created an environment that allows people to be motivated, the lack of desire to do the job is the employee's fault. If someone isn't the motivated type, there's not much you can do to change him or her.

Before we began advertising our company in 1994, we invested heavily in employee training for our firm. We created extensive manuals on everything from how to answer the phone to how to write a letter closing a file, and everything in between. We gave our case managers private offices when we could and we treated them like the paraprofessionals we wanted them to be. Case managers weren't lawyers, but they were not lowly staff who could be abused by the lawyers, either. While we couldn't pay our employees the highest wages in the market, we invested in them through our offices and training, along with building the business. We communicated that they could grow along with us, and they did. Today, we still continue these traditions, offering our employees access to online classes, college tuition reimbursement programs, and in-office training. Investing in our employees through training and developing a culture of respect, growth, and shared success has created a clear competitive advantage for us.

I knew all along my employees would be our greatest assets. People want lawyers to be more approachable. They want to attend meetings in comfortable offices, not in places in which elite law experts can lord legal knowledge over them. We understood that it is the shared attitude that makes employees buy into a company's vision, especially in a service business.

When I first started my business, I wanted all of my employees to be as passionate about the firm as I was. That was a mistake and a precursor to heartache. There is no way, not in any organization, you can get everybody to be as passionate as the leader must be. Instead, as a leader, you should seek to make people more passionate about their work or the organization's goals; if you think you can get everyone to feel the same passion you do, you are deluding yourself.

What you must do is find ways to line up what makes your employees passionate with your organization's goals. You must line up their wins with your win.

Sometimes matching up those wins can be challenging. One lawyer in our firm, Frank Hallstrom, is a rare specimen: he's smart beyond what most of us other lawyers could ever hope for and can remember aspects of the law that we never could. However, growing the firm or handling more cases so he could make more money was not his passion. He was not against the firm growing. He did a fantastic job for our clients, and he provided us with a huge mental resource. However, his passions were elsewhere: they included Scouting and, as a part of Scouting, hiking the Appalachian Trail.

To develop our win-win, I laid out a plan for success that he endorsed and accepted. After he completed the plan, we would give him several months off, paid, so he could walk the Appalachian Trail. Through this plan, Frank and I found a way to take the company's goals and link them with his passions so we all could win.

Frank earned that time off. Then, remaining true to the unique man he is, he chose not to walk the trail but to give back instead. You see, when Frank was in the service, long before he entered law school, he had stopped over in Morocco. There, the specter of four-, five- and six-year-old homeless throwaway kids seared into his mind and haunted him. He decided that instead of walking the trail, he would give back to those kids, so he went to Morocco and worked with at-risk kids to give them a better chance in life. This great thing he did still fills me with pride and emotion, and our firm had a small part in that great thing because we found a way to join his passions with ours.

People's passions are powerful. If you are in an organization, you should strive mightily to adopt the passions of that organization or find a way to link your passions to theirs. If you are the leader, you should model that passion, and you should also find ways to link others' passions to those you have set for the group.

HOW DO I FIND MY PASSION?

"Okay," you might be saying now. "I get it. If I want to give myself the best opportunity to be successful in whatever endeavor I choose, I need to have passion. I can have multiple reasons to win, and not everybody in my organization has to have the same ones I do. I need to minimize the bad fear we may all have, I need to make sure the good fear I have is not overbearing, and I need to balance my passion with all parts of my life. If I am in an organization, I need to help others find and maximize their passions, too. Whew! That's a tall order. How the heck do I find my passions?"

To answer this question, let's step back to Rule One. We talked about sitting alone and thinking about what it is you want. Now, do the same thing to figure out *why* you want what you want. What is important in your life and in your heart? What gives you joy? When do you feel maximized, alive, and energized? Take an inventory of what you spend your time doing. Either you will find your passion or you will find what holds you back. Are you living a life of quiet desperation, or are you marching toward those things you hold dear? Too many people just float, exist, and live on a day-to-day basis. They are so worried about missing the mark that they choose to ignore and avoid their passions. In return, they get a lifeless life; they get the feeling that the best is passing them by. The sad thing is, they're right. Achieving a real life, a fully lived life, comes from your passion and from your heart.

> ### GOLDEN NUGGET
> *What is important in your life and in your heart? What gives you joy? When do you feel maximized, alive, and energized? Take an inventory of what you spend your time doing. Either you will find your passion or you will find what holds you back.*
>
>

I wish so much I could wave a wand over you and find this passion for you. I wish I could scan you in an MRI machine, and this passion would reveal itself. Unfortunately, we can't do that. Only you can find this passion inside yourself, and doing so is hard work. If you work consistently to figure out yourself and your life, you give yourself a better chance to see the true you and the passions that can drive you. Are you seeing the trend here? As I've said before, you can use these rules to accomplish anything, even to figure out the rules themselves.

PASSION IS NOT ENOUGH

Being in the ring is not enough. Seeing the end first and having a passion for the endeavor is not enough, either. The most critical part of following Rule Three is you must be present *in the moment* with your positive mental attitude: that will to win, the will to be successful, and the will in which failure is not an option.

A skeptic might say, "Wait a minute. Didn't you say that sometimes you have to cut your losses and move on?"

Yes, I did. However, there is a difference between living life with the will to win and living with the goal of ultimately succeeding in every endeavor.

I can't tell you how many times over the years I have heard somebody say, "Yeah, I'm going to open up a store and see how it goes." My all-time favorite, which I once heard a client say, is this: "Sure, we've had a lot of problems, but I'm gonna marry him and see if that'll fix it."

Are you kidding me? Yet many people live their lives by this approach, thinking, "Let's just give it a try and see what happens."

Most people who operate this way have no commitment to success. They use this trying-it-out attitude as a psychological out, a safety valve for when the endeavor fails to meet expectations. Notice I didn't say if the endeavor fails to meet *goals*. If you live your life or operate your business according to this approach, you really don't have goals. At best, you have an expectation, and that expectation is probably more for failure than success.

Kenneth Blanchard, author of the famous *One-Minute Manager* books, said it this way: "There's a difference between interest and commitment. When you're interested in doing something, you do it only when it's convenient. When you're committed to something, you accept no excuses, only results."

The will to win is so important to success. It is important to life, too. Many scholars have written about the mortality rate differences between medical patients who have a strong will to survive and those who do not. You see this drive in movies and TV shows, too: "Don't quit on me," a character will plead, "don't give up, don't die on me." The will to live and the will to win are strong and powerful. This type of will to live can overcome obstacles, whether they are self-inflicted or just plain old accidents.

> **GOLDEN NUGGET**
>
> *The will to live and the will to win are strong and powerful. This type of will to live can overcome obstacles, whether they are self-inflicted or just plain old accidents.*

Many great people have talked about this desire to win as a crucial aspect for success. Let's consider a few standout remarks:

The will to win, the desire to succeed, the urge to reach your full potential...These are the keys that will unlock the door to personal excellence.

–Confucius

I play to win, whether during practice or a real game. And I will not let anything get in the way of me and my competitive enthusiasm to win.

−Michael Jordan

My philosophy of life is that if we make up our mind what we are going to make of our lives, then work hard toward that goal, we never lose—somehow we win out.

−Ronald Reagan

Winning is not a sometime thing; it's an all the time thing. You don't win once in a while, you don't do things right once in a while, you do them right all the time. Winning is habit. Unfortunately, so is losing.

−Vince Lombardi

Every person who wins in any undertaking must be willing to cut all sources of retreat. Only by doing so can one be sure of maintaining that state of mind known as a burning desire to win— essential to success.

−Napoleon Hill

Sustaining the will to win, that part of Rule Three, is the hardest of these rules for me to live by each and every day. I know my passions and I embrace them. I am an ideas guy and I love to plan. I will work very hard, not only on the planning, but the tasks as well. At a core level, I understand consistent competency is the true way to achieve all-the-time excellence. I know that every day I must have the will to win. Yet for me, given my personality, this last requirement is the hardest. This one goes against my nature, and this is the one about which I must be constantly vigilant.

I suspect this is the case for most people because of similar reasons. Our emotions and personalities get in the way. To summon up the courage and the will every single day to do what we know we must do is tough. It's difficult, just like the title of this book says. Yet we must.

SUMMONING ELVIS AND THE WILL TO WIN

I love Elvis. I love his music and, yes, I admit I love his movies. (Rumor has it there may even be pictures of me dressed as Elvis for a charitable fundraiser. "Thank you. Thank you very much.")

When he went on stage, Elvis struggled with the courage and the will to wow his audience. He and some of his staff would pace his dressing room before a show, repeating mantras like, "You are the king of rock and roll. This is your audience and your stage. You are a star and you will be a star tonight."

These positive affirmations helped Elvis overcome his mental obstacles. However, these weren't just sloppy, positive-thinking clichés. He practiced his craft, his songs, and his moves, and he rehearsed the shows. Elvis knew that without the right mental attitude *in the moment*, all his work, all that consistent competency, would often be for naught.

My daughter Jamie, who's currently singing in Nashville, learned this lesson early on in her singing career. She was making an appearance at a fundraiser sponsored by a radio station. They had done tons of advertising, and she expected a throng of people.

That throng turned out to be fewer than ten. There were lots of empty seats. Jamie was devastated, so she didn't perform. Well, she went on stage and she sang, but she didn't perform. She knew it, and we knew it. Afterward, she said she didn't see the point since there were so few people in the audience.

What a great time, at the early stage of her career, for her to learn a very valuable lesson. She had gone into the ring without the will to win. She had judged her effort by the size of the ring instead of the size of her ability. Ultimately, she knew she had let herself and her audience down.

Today, you won't see that in her. Her new mantra is "five or five thousand, they are getting the whole show!" Like Elvis, Jamie talks to herself before a show and gets her mind ready for the performance. She has learned that the will to win in the moment—in *each* moment—is critical if she wants all her hard work and consistent competency to pay off.

We see the same thing with salespeople at conventions and with athletes doing their pre-game "mental up" exercises; in both cases, folks are getting mentally prepared for the battle ahead. Sam Walton of Wal-Mart, for example, was legendary for his daily pre-opening pep rallies.

Sometimes we just need a mental kick in the pants—or even a simple mental push—to help us get that will to win where it needs to be.

BE LIKE ELVIS AND JAMIE

I have used these little techniques to help me get that will to win, that attitude each moment demands, in two areas: in life and in business.

Let me share two examples of how I used these techniques in business. First, I used to love the courtroom, but I also hated it. So much was on the line for my clients. Would I measure up? I developed a routine of getting to the courtroom at least thirty minutes before anyone else. I would walk between the counsel tables, the jury box, and the witness stand. I would tell myself out loud, mimicking Elvis,

"This is my courtroom; this is where I belong. I have prepared my case; I have done the work; I know the facts, the law, and my client. I am ready." In each case, these few moments of mental reflection and readiness helped calm my nerves, focus my thoughts, and steel me for the day that would unfold.

Second, I learned I had to manage the times in which I walk across the parking lot from my car to the office. Typically, I wear my emotions on my sleeve. If a day was going badly, it showed on my face the moment I walked into the office. Because of that, I was not giving my people the leadership they needed and deserved.

I'm not saying a leader should never show anxiousness or concern; instead, the emotions of the day should be more balanced. In times of real trouble, a leader needs to lead in action and in the important intangibles.

One day, Teresa, who still worked with me at the firm, took me aside and said, "You have to quit this. You have to find a way between the car and the office door to become the leader we all need."

You see, she is a major part of my accountability system.

Here is what I did then and still do to this day. When I arrive at my office, I turn off the car and take a moment to check in with myself and with my attitude. I get my attitude right before I walk in the door. I am happy to report this method works most of the time. We are all human; we are all going to have rough spots. Our will may be weak from time to time, but we need to check it and fix it, especially if we are acting as leaders. Sometimes as I pull the car into the driveway when getting home in the evening, I need to do the same thing. I need to get my attitude right before I walk into my home. There I need to have the will to win, and to be present in the moment, as a husband and father.

I recently saw this concept illustrated with an interesting mathematical formula that equates the letters of the alphabet to numbers. Suppose A equals 1, B equals 2, C equals 3, and so on, all the way up through Z equaling 26. Using that bit of code, we can calculate the Three Rules' importance as percentages:

$$H + A + R + D + W + O + R + K$$
$$8 + 1 + 18 + 4 + 23 + 15 + 18 + 11 = 98\%$$

$$K + N + O + W + L + E + D + G + E$$
$$11 + 14 + 15 + 23 + 12 + 5 + 4 + 7 + 5 = 96\%$$

Both of these are important. However, all by itself Rule One (hard work) falls just a little short of 100 percent. Rule Two's competency (knowledge) falls a little bit shorter of the goal. Yet Rule Three (attitude), which is the will to win every day you step into the ring, gets a perfect score:

$$A + T + T + I + T + U + D + E$$
$$1 + 20 + 20 + 9 + 20 + 21 + 4 + 5 = 100\%$$

LEARNING THE RIGHT ATTITUDE

Vince Lombardi said winning is a habit. That means it can be learned, practiced, and lost, just like any other skill.

This is great news. If we don't have that winning attitude or that passion today, our future is not lost. We can still get, find, and practice that attitude, and it can become a habit for us. Lombardi knew his players could practice winning attitudes and desires just like they could practice how to block and tackle. The will to win is not a gift from the gods that you either have or you don't. Instead, it is a gift to yourself. Either you can cultivate, grow, and practice, so this gift leads you forward, or you can leave it to wilt on the vine along with your hopes and desires.

Lombardi's statement also means the opposite is true. Losing can be a habit. The difference between the habits of winning and losing is all in the attitude we want and the work we do to practice and support that attitude.

How do we get this good attitude? How do we keep it on a consistent basis?

If you want to succeed in your efforts to develop a good attitude, why don't you use the Three Rules?

First, see the end, or the goal, and determine what attitude you need to reach it. At work, I want to have an attitude that's supportive, yet demands we give our clients the work they deserve. At home, I want to have an attitude that's loving, yet demands we give each other and ourselves the peaceful environment we deserve.

See the trend here?

Once you've established the attitude you want, you can work at developing those parts of your personality and heart that stand in the way. We learn to be consistently competent in these attitudes by practicing them (for example, as in my habit of stopping before I get out of the car to do a "check up from the neck up"). Always go into this ring of attitude-building with the will to win and the will to succeed.

HELP YOUR ATTITUDE BY ELIMINATING RETREAT

We have seen the end first and know our passions. Check. We have balanced those passions and developed them. Check. We have found some little techniques we can use to help us keep that great attitude and hold on to our will to win in the moment. Big check!

But sometimes that just ain't enough.

Napoleon Hill, author of *Think and Grow Rich* and one of the fathers of personal success literature, said, "Cut all sources of retreat." Why did he make this statement, which is about attitude? He understood that our present-moment will to win is critical and yet difficult to achieve on a day-to-day basis. He knew that even with your hard work and your consistent competency leading you to sustained excellence, you'd find some days too tough and some valleys too deep. If you gave in to those feelings, you would forget that you even had a passion, let alone what it is.

Dr. Hill knew that if you cut off your avenues of retreat, you take away your escape routes and outs that you'd be tempted to turn to when the going gets tough. By eliminating retreats, you actually bolster your attitude and your will to win because you have no choice. You have the original choice to cut off those sources of retreat, but once you make the decision and make those cuts, you simply have to succeed.

You have gotten to know my youngest daughter Jamie, the talented singer, a little in this book. What you don't yet know is that Jamie recently completed law school. She wanted to go to Nashville and begin her music career right after she received her law school acceptance. However, after weighing the options, she decided finishing her education first was best. In addition to her familiarity with the law (generated from her family and high school experience), she also knew that the music business is centered around contracts, interstate sales, international royalties, and potential liability when things on a stage go wrong.

Still, this decision was not easy for her. Though intellectually she knew it was the right thing to do, Jamie's passion and refuge is music. She wanted to be in Nashville, but she understood that "to everything there is a season." So, she marched on. She started a band and performed some weekends (once they even performed for her law school), and she spent her summers in Nashville writing songs with some of the best writers in the world.

Yet during those long, hard days of class and endless amounts of reading, several times Jamie needed a "check up from the neck up." At other times, she needed to have a "bitch and moan" session. In those cases, that's just what we did.

Jamie made it through three long, tough years of law school. (Don't you just love how the importance of the number three thing keeps popping up?) She graduated from law school in the spring of 2012, and then she moved to Tennessee and began to prepare for her six weeks of study before the bar exam.

At that point, Jamie did something very smart. She cut off her avenues of retreat. She cut off access to Facebook and she cut off music. She eliminated those things she enjoyed so she could commit herself to one last push and achieve that last hurdle. She knew if those things were still in her life during those six weeks of studying, they would be places to which she could retreat. She would be able to go to these places to soothe her attitude, to stroke her passion, and to salve her need to be onstage. When our kids or our employees do something really great and really cool without prodding, sometimes we simply know that they have gotten it—what we've been trying to instill in them—and that they are going to be okay. During those six weeks, Jamie put into practice an important technique that helped her keep her attitude in the right place, even though everything within her wanted to chuck it all and get back up on that stage. She understands that you don't always naturally have the will to win in the moment; instead, sometimes you have to cut off your avenues of retreat in order to keep your attitude where it needs to be.

When Teresa and I were developing our law firm, we had a similar moment in which we had to cut off our pathways to retreat, too. Our firm was growing fast. Too fast. Our advertising was working, the processes were working, and we were working ourselves to death. So we made the choice to go all in and put it all on the line.

We had started the firm with just a $3,500 loan from a bank. Now we were on TV and growing. I needed lawyers and I needed good ones quickly. I developed a plan to ask the bank for a $150,000 loan. This amount was enough to secure a big chunk of three lawyers' salaries for a year. The bank agreed, but only after we personally guaranteed the loan. The bank took a second mortgage on our house and wrapped up all our finances tightly.

We had no avenues of retreat. That was it. We learned and experienced what Dr. Hill taught. Sometimes, but only sometimes, your back needs to be up against a wall to keep your attitude in the right position.

Not once in this book, or in any other book I have ever read, has an author said you need to cut off avenues of retreat so you will work harder, take the time to determine necessary competencies, or finally find what excellence means. No. That strong and decisive step is reserved for your attitude, your will to win. Dr. Hill knew what we all must learn. Our attitude, our will to win in that moment is of singular importance and is singularly difficult.

Selectively retreating, making winning into a habit, and fostering your will to win are all about your attitude and passion.

> **GOLDEN NUGGET**
> *Selectively retreating, making winning into a habit, and fostering your will to win are all about your attitude and passion.*

They're about discovering *why*: about answering the questions posed in Rule Three.

CELEBRATE VICTORIES AND HONOR THOSE WHO SUCCEED

One of my favorite movies is *Rudy*, which is about Rudy, a blue-collar, steel-mill kid who dreamed about going to Notre Dame to play football. Rudy was undersized and under-talented. Notre Dame was, well, Notre Dame. However, Rudy had some things that really mattered. He had heart, he had passion, he had the ability and the willingness to get up when he was knocked down, and he did not know the meaning of the word *quit*. Oh, he wanted to quit sometimes, but he always summoned within himself the courage and the heart to see his goal through.

After all his years of hard work and all his efforts to become consistently competent, Rudy is finally let into the game. That scene alone makes for a good movie script, and a good lesson for us all, but I want to look at that final scene a little differently.

The fans and the other players want Rudy in the game. However, the coach wants to win, which he thinks he can do with his best on the field. Perhaps he also does not want the other coaches in the league to see he has an undersized and under-talented guy on his team, so he is reluctant to let Rudy play. The crowd and the players start to chant, "Rudy, Rudy." Finally, the coach relents and puts Rudy in. Rudy fulfills his goal and accomplishes his mission.

The real message of that moment, I believe, is the effect Rudy has on the rest of his team. They did not just want him in the game; they needed him in that game. They didn't need him there in order to win, though. Instead, they needed him there to validate all the work he had done. They needed to honor him, to acknowledge his efforts, and to reward him, their teammate who had given so much to his dream and to their team.

Who is the Rudy in your company? Who is the Rudy in your family? Who is giving it all with, perhaps, less talent? Are you honoring and celebrating the successes of your people, all of your people? While you are investigating, are you taking the time to honor and value your own successes too? I'm preaching to myself here when I ask these questions. If you want sustained, long-term success, you must celebrate those little wins along the way. You don't need to spend a long time and become a one-hit wonder, but you do need to savor them—or, as my good friend Steve Gilliland would say, "You need to enjoy the ride!"

The will to win is so critical. It's a habit and a choice, and you can develop it. It is not a talent or a gift with which you are born. You can create and develop your will to win. You can use techniques to help you "check up from the neck up" when the moment demands it. When the time comes, you must be ready to put your back up against that wall.

You can do it. You must.

> **GOLDEN NUGGET**
> *The will to win is so critical. It's a habit and a choice, and you can develop it. It is not a talent or a gift with which you are born. You can create and develop your will to win.*
>
>

CHEATING ISN'T WINNING

With all this talk about winning and the will to win in the moment, I want to say a few words about ethics and the desire to win at any cost. Winning by cheating, via losing your ethical way, through selfishness and greed, or at the expense of others is not winning at all. It is losing on all levels. You must be willing to pay the price of success in putting yourself through the hardness and difficulty of the Three Rules, but you should never sell your soul for success. As the Bible puts it, "For what should it profit a man if he gains the whole world and loses his own soul?"

We have all seen too many stories about people who cheated and hurt others just to make themselves look successful. Their names will remain on the trash heap of history, forever linked to the evils and pain they created. None of us is a saint. Well, I know I am not. I am not trying to be holier than anyone. Whether that cheating involves taking steroids, cooking the books, lying to clients, or just plain old cutting the corners, it's still cheating. True success is earned, not stolen.

Make sure the end you see first includes your ability to look in the mirror and hold your head up high, both proud and humble that you achieved your goals with integrity.

FINAL THOUGHTS

Hard work will eventually pay off.
Consistent competency is better than erratic excellence.
Never go into the ring without the will to win.

By 2005, when Jamie graduated high school, Teresa and I had met and exceeded our family business plan's three financial goals. We had succeeded.

So, was that it? After all, we had met our goals. No, that wasn't it. It was time for new goals. Remember, sometimes life throws unexpected curves at you. Whether you're working toward your current goals, developing new goals, or reworking a plan due to a change in circumstances outside your control, you can always abide by and challenge yourself with the Three Rules.

Not long after Teresa and I had reached that goal and noted our success, we encountered this little thing called a *recession* that started in 2008. That year, the real estate market took a major tumble. We didn't foresee this back in 2005 when we planned to expand our law firm into South Carolina and develop more real estate projects. We'd even started a recycling business that concentrated on green and concrete waste from development projects, which was a natural expansion for us.

As if that pressure wasn't enough, in 2008 I ran for North Carolina's State Attorney General. As the Republican nominee, I headed to the general election. If elected, I decided, I would sell the entire law firm to a team of our lawyers. If I didn't win? I didn't plan for that; obviously, I entered the political ring with the will to win.

To say that 2008 was not the best of year for my family and our business would be an understatement. Of course, as a Republican in 2008, I lost the election. Teresa and I managed to create a high note in the midst of this by selling a portion of the firm to a group of our lawyers. However, with the destruction of the national real estate market and the depths of the worst economy since the Great Depression, my companies all experienced the same tough times that others faced.

Yet I didn't move back in with my in-laws, and I didn't take up a new career in pizza delivery.

By the end of 2007, we had grown to more than fifteen offices and 130 employees. As the recession kicked in, the law firm's volume of cases swung wildly from month to month. The recycling business went almost eighteen months with no new contracts to even bid on as real estate development in North Carolina screeched to a halt. In the ensuing years, we have significantly curtailed our law firm's efforts in South Carolina and closed the recycling company. We have struggled for more than four years to keep our real estate holdings alive while treading water on our undeveloped parcels.

In the midst of these troubles, though, there are positives. Our management team at the firm has taken great steps to refocus the company on efficiencies and to broaden the types of cases we handle. By selling equipment and some of our real estate, we significantly pared down the real estate business's debt and refocused the business, making it even stronger.

In 2010, we took my longtime hobby and passion, songwriting, and opened a music publishing company in Nashville. This company is seeing significant positive signs.

I didn't create the real estate or banking problems; neither did any businessperson I know. However, these problems have adversely affected our lives, as well as the lives of thousands of small-business owners and employees. The big boys who caused the problems received billions in bailouts, while job-creating small businesses were cut off from bank loans and access to capital.

Through it all, our companies, and the vast majority of other small companies, have struggled through. In some cases, they have soared through.

> **GOLDEN NUGGET**
>
> *The big boys who caused the problems received billions in bailouts, while job-creating small businesses were cut off from bank loans and access to capital.*

Our companies' executives are smarter and more experienced today than they were four years ago. They are more focused and more determined to wait this bad economy out and to grow our companies. Over the years, I have been so proud of them because of our company's growth and our commitment to our clients. Today, I'm even more proud as they enter the ring each day with the will to win, steeled for and dedicated to prospering in a tough economy.

I hope by now you realize these three simple yet difficult rules can be used everywhere and in all aspects of your life. They are not limited to business or sports. You can even use the rules to develop the habits, attitudes, and work ethic you need to implement the rules themselves. By their very nature, they are easy to remember, easy to memorize, and easy to use as a mantra. I bet you can say the Three Rules in order and correctly. Try it!

If you commit these Three Rules of success to memory, they will be with you and at the top of your mind every day. I often see others effectively using at least one of the rules in my everyday life, whether they know the rules or not. I challenge you to make the rules part of your daily life as well. It is so exciting to experience those simple, quiet moments when you know you can improve your chances for success in whatever endeavor you choose just by knowing and using these rules.

As you get to know the rules and explore how to implement them in your life, share them with others. By teaching, we learn. By sharing these rules and our goals, we can build accountability systems.

At a recent yoga session, my instructor said, "Tell me again how that competency one goes. I was trying to tell my husband."

Later that day, I was going too fast for a particular pose, and she said, "Slow down. Remember, consistent competency is better than erratic excellence." I almost fell out of the pose laughing.

Have fun with the Three Rules. Make them a game. Try to spot them in your life and in others' lives. Yet take their message seriously. Deciding what you want is not a one-time thing. Sometimes, it can seem like a lifetime thing. While deciding what you want and going after it can change your life, what you want may change as you move through life's stages. When you enter a new venture, recheck the necessary core competencies and do an inventory of what you need to add to your repertoire.

Finally, create processes in your life that will help you retain your passions and keep your attitude about success and winning where it needs to be in each moment.

In closing, I have three wishes for you:

I wish for you to see the end first.

I wish for you hard work, consistent competency, and the will to win.

I wish for you the joy of success and many days of memorable excellence.

See THE END first!

ACKNOWLEDGEMENTS

Wow. I have tried multiple times to write this part of the book and, quite frankly, I would never have guessed it would be this hard. It's not hard to know who has helped me so much over the years, who has meant so much to me and to my family, or who has helped me finish my first book. What is so hard is typing through the emotions, through the tears and through laughter as I replay so many events in my life. Here goes…

First I want to thank my family. My mom and dad, Jane and Bob, gave their children a loving and caring home; they always told us we could do and be what we wanted and were willing to work hard to achieve. I owe so much to them and to my sister and brothers. My parents-in-law, Nancy and Harold, and their entire family have always loved us. They took us in when we were at our lowest point, and I will always be grateful.

I thank Teresa, who is so private and so perceptive; Brandi, who has such a big heart and could sell ice to Eskimos; and Jamie, who has so much native talent and always looks first to the goodness in all people. Each of you let me pursue my dreams, did not let me drown in a sea of estrogen, and let me open our lives to the world in this book.

To my longtime friends, Marshall Hurley and Robb Grindstaff, thank you for being my friends; thank you, too, for bringing your talents in photography and in the written word to my efforts to complete this book.

To our other friends who have shared so much of our lives, thank you for supporting us through the years and loving us through it all.

To our employees and to our business partners, I acknowledge you, your hard work, and your commitment to our clients and companies. To my friends and mentors in the business world, thank you for helping me find my way and for lifting me up when I needed it most.

To Steve Gilliland, thank you for befriending and encouraging me; thank you, too, for your willingness to honor me by writing this book's foreword.

To those who have read and endorsed our message, thank you for your friendship and your willingness to help.

Finally, to all the other authors out there whose books and tapes I have devoured, I acknowledge you and thank you. Sometimes it is hard to know where your thoughts end and mine begin. I hope I have appropriately given you credit throughout this book because you and your words have meant so much to me.

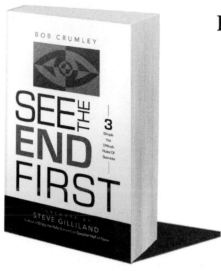

How can you use this book?

MOTIVATE

EDUCATE

THANK

INSPIRE

PROMOTE

CONNECT

Why have a custom version of *See the End First*?

- Build personal bonds with customers, prospects, employees, donors, and key constituencies
- Develop a long-lasting reminder of your event, milestone, or celebration
- Provide a keepsake that inspires change in behavior and change in lives
- Deliver the ultimate "thank you" gift that remains on coffee tables and bookshelves
- Generate the "wow" factor

Books are thoughtful gifts that provide a genuine sentiment that other promotional items cannot express. They promote employee discussions and interaction, reinforce an event's meaning or location, and they make a lasting impression. Use your book to say "Thank You" and show people that you care.